THE CHILD'S
STORY BIBLE:
OLD TESTAMENT

Volume 1—Genesis to Ruth

The Child's Story Bible:
Old Testament

Volume 1—Genesis to Ruth

Catherine F. Vos

*New edition
illustrated in full colour
by Betty Beeby*

THE BANNER OF TRUTH TRUST

THE BANNER OF TRUTH TRUST
3 Murrayfield Road, Edinburgh EH12 6EL
PO Box 621, Carlisle, Pennsylvania 17013, USA

*

THE CHILD'S STORY BIBLE
by CATHERINE F. VOS

Entire contents, including illustrations,
Copyright 1935, 1949, 1958, and 1969 by
WM. B. EERDMANS PUBLISHING COMPANY
Grand Rapids, Michigan, U.S.A.

Vol. 1, November, 1934
Vol. 2, October, 1935
Vol. 3, October, 1936
One-volume edition, April, 1940
Second edition, August, 1949
Third edition, May, 1958
Fourth edition, October, 1969

This English edition is published by special arrangement with
Wm. B. Eerdmans Publishing Company
Grand Rapids, Michigan, U.S.A.

1969

New Testament only
Reprinted 1976

Old Testament: Genesis to Ruth
Reprinted 1977
Reprinted 1984
Reprinted 1998

ISBN 0 85151 250 X

Printed in Great Britain by
The Bath Press, Bath

Dedication

To My Dear Mother in Heaven,
Who Told Me These Stories
When I Was a Little Child,
In Much the Same Way
In Which I Have Written Them
In This Book.

Foreword

Retelling Bible stories is both a painstaking and a rewarding task. By the use of simple and dignified language the author, Mrs. Catherine F. Vos, has in her book preserved the beauty of the biblical narratives and at the same time skilfully brought out the meaning of the scriptural account. Her picturesque, imaginative, and poetic style is in harmony with the dignity of the message.

For such reasons the *Child's Story Bible* is one of the most widely known and used Bible story books. The National Union of Christian Schools is happy to have had a hand in the preparation of this book, which was originally intended for use in the Christian schools. Teachers use it for Bible instruction in primary and intermediate grades.

Parents find that the material is adapted also for home use: for reading to the children and also for placing in their hands for personal reading. Although it is intended primarily for children from seven to twelve years of age, it is eminently suitable for reading to those of a much younger age and it is valued by adults as a Bible history.

The publishers spared no expense to make this volume beautiful and to make it appealing to the child. Large, readable type and full-colour art work, help to make it an attractive book. A new element in this edition is the reproduction of several oil paintings of principal Bible characters.

Telling the story of salvation to those who come after us is a glorious task. Christian faith has its roots in historical events. We trust that the *Child's Story Bible* may be a guide to the authoritative narration of these events, the Book of books, and to Him who said, "I am the way, the truth, and the life."

JOHN A. VANDER ARK, *Director*
National Union of Christian Schools

TABLE OF CONTENTS

Old Testament: Genesis to Ruth

CONTENTS

CONTENTS

CHAPTER 1

In the Beginning God

PART 1 — GOD IS AND WAS

Long, long ago — nobody knows how long ago — this world on which we live, this big ball that we call earth, was not here. The earth did not exist. There was nothing but emptiness, wide empty space. That was before the beginning of the first things, before the beginning of time.

Yet there was something in that long, long ago. God was there.

When did God begin? And who made God?

No one made God. And God did not begin. God has always been. Forever and ever and ever, God has lived. God never had a beginning, and His life will never end.

If you were to take a cup and dip water out of the big wide and deep ocean, you could dip and dip and dip but you could never dip the ocean dry. Your mind is like a little cup, and God's life is like the big deep ocean. You cannot dip the ocean dry with a cup. And we cannot understand God's life, that never began, and will never, never end.

Some day the sun and moon and stars, and the earth on which we live, will all grow old, just as your clothes grow old and worn out. But God will be the same as He was, today and yesterday and long, long ago. His life will go on and on, forever.

God is eternal.

God is also wonderful and very great. He can do many things which men cannot do.

We can be in only one place at a time. If we want to be in some other place, we have to go there. But God is in Heaven, and at the same time He is everywhere upon earth.

If we go into the deepest dark mines, God is there.

If we fly up into the clouds of the sky, God is there.

God sees us always, and everywhere. He knows everything that we do, hears every word that we speak, and even knows the thoughts that we have in our minds.

We cannot hide from God. If we do wrong, God knows it, even if we have not told anyone. He knows, too, when we have tried to be good and to please Him, even if no one else knows.

Long ago someone said: *Thou God seest me* (Genesis 16:13). That is a good line to remember.

God is even more wonderful. He knows everything that is going to happen in the world. We do not know what will happen tomorrow. But God knows everything. He knows what is going to happen to-morrow, and next week, and next year, and always, till the very end of the world. God also knows what will happen after the world has passed away.

And God is good. He is perfectly good, so that He cannot do anything wrong. Everything that God does is right.

Then too, God is love. He loves you more than anyone in the world loves you. He loves you more than even your father and your mother love you. It was God who gave you a father and mother to love you and take care of you.

Your father and mother, much as they love you, cannot take care of you all the time. Sometimes they must be absent. At night they must sleep.

But God is always near you, and He is always taking care of you. God never sleeps. All night long, when you are sleeping, God is watching over you and caring for you. God takes care of you all of the day-time too.

It is God who made you. He made you because He wanted to love a child just like you. God wants you to love Him too.

Heaven is God's home. Heaven is more beautiful than any place you have ever seen. It is more beautiful than anything you can imagine.

There is a wonderful river in Heaven called the River of the Water of Life, with water clear as crystal.

There is no sickness nor sadness in Heaven, but all is joy and happiness. There are no tears. There is no crying. There is no death.

There is no dark night in Heaven, but always bright beautiful day. They do not need the light of the sun there, for the glory of God makes Heaven brighter than the sun.

God lives in Heaven. And with Him there are the beautiful angels, thousands and thousands of them.

With Him, too, are all the good people who have died.

And there is a place there for us, if we love God and our sins are forgiven for Jesus' sake.

PART 2 — THE ANGELS, GOOD AND BAD

God made the beautiful angels to live with Him in Heaven.

The angels are bright like the light. They are much stronger than men, and can do things that men cannot do. They go where God sends them. They can fly down from Heaven to this earth.

These angels love God and are happy. They spend all their time loving and praising God, and doing whatever He wants them to do.

There are very many angels, so many that we cannot count them — ten thousand times ten thousand, and thousands of thousands.

Some are called arch-angels, because they are greater than the rest. God has let us know the names of a few. There is the great arch-angel Gabriel, who stands in God's holy presence. God has sent him down to earth several times, with messages from God to man. It was the arch-angel Gabriel who told Mary that God was going to send the baby Jesus to her.

Sometimes God sends angels down to earth to help people who are in trouble. An angel once opened the prison door to let God's servant Peter out. The Bible tells of more than twenty times that God sent angels down to earth with messages to men.

But, long ago, there were some angels in Heaven who turned away from being good. Instead of loving God, they began to hate Him. They became wicked.

The name of the leader of these wicked angels is Satan. Many other angels listened to Satan and were wicked like Him.

There can be nothing wicked in God's beautiful Heaven. So God cast out the wicked angels. Now they are no longer called angels. They are called demons.

The demons hate everything that is good. Most of all they hate God. And they do not want us to love Him, or to be good, and go to live with Him in Heaven after we die. They try in every possible way to make us wicked like themselves. They want us to lie and steal, to be disobedient and cross and cruel.

But they are afraid of God. God is much stronger than Satan and all his demons. They fear and tremble before Him.

So we need not to be afraid of them, though they are very strong. But we should serve God, as the good angels do, and try in every way to please Him. Let us pray to God always. He will take care of us. He will help us and make us strong to do the good.

CHAPTER 2

How the World Began

GENESIS 1

"In the beginning God created the heavens and the earth."

If we did not have the Bible to tell us that long ago, *in the beginning*, God created the earth, we would have no way of knowing who made it.

Created means *made out of nothing*.

When a man makes a house, he must first have some wood of which to build it, and some nails, and some glass for windows. If he does not have something of which to make it, he cannot build a house.

But God made the world out of nothing at all.

God made the world in a most wonderful way. When God began to make the world, He did not have to work hard and long, as a man has to work when he makes a house. All God had to do was simply to speak and the world began.

But God did not make the world all at once as we see it now.

At first land and water, air and sky were all mixed up, without any shape. Over it all was darkness — deep, deep darkness, without a ray of light.

"Then God said, 'Let there be light,' and there was light.

"And God saw the light, that it was good, and God divided the light from the darkness. And God called the light Day, and the darkness He called Night."

That was the very first day.

It is God who still makes the daylight come every morning, so that we can get up out of our beds to work and play. It is God, too, who sends the darkness every night, so that we can sleep quietly, and rest our tired bodies.

We need never be afraid of the darkness, because it is God's darkness. He made it and He will not let anything hurt us.

God made the air and the blue sky with the soft white clouds floating in it, on the second day.

The earth and the water were still mixed up. After God made the air and the blue sky, God said: *"Let the waters under the heavens be gathered together unto one place, and let the dry land appear."*

The waters obeyed God. They separated themselves from the earth and ran down the hills into the valleys and out into the sea.

So the deep places of the earth were filled with water, and the big oceans began to appear. The land — the hills and the mountains — stood up high and dry above the oceans.

"And God called the dry land Earth and the gathering together of the waters He called Seas. And God saw that it was good."

Now there was light, and the beautiful blue sky. There were hills, valleys, plains, brooks, rivers, and oceans. The world was ready for something to grow on it.

Then God commanded the earth to bring forth grass and vegetables and fruit trees.

As soon as God had said it, the bare earth began to grow green with beautiful grass. Bright colored flowers began to spring up everywhere. All kinds of vegetables began to grow.

Peaches, apples, oranges, and cherries, all these delicious fruits were created by God at this time.

This was when God made the first roses and lilies, and all the other flowers which make the world very beautiful.

"And God saw that it was good. And there was evening and there was morning, a third day."

Next, God made the great and glorious sun to flood the earth with beautiful sunshine and make the earth warm, so that all the flowers, fruits, and plants could grow.

God also made the silver moon to shine in the dark night when the sun has gone away.

God made also the thousands and thousands of bright twinkling stars that shine in the sky at night.

The sun, the moon, and the stars God made on the fourth day. And God saw that it was good.

Now that the beautiful earth was clothed with grass and flowers and trees, and the warm sun was pouring down upon it, it was ready for some animals to live on it.

The first living creatures that God made were fishes and birds.

God filled the brooks and rivers and the mighty ocean with all kinds of fishes — great whales and little minnows, and every kind of fish that swims.

God made all the beautiful, sweet-singing birds at this time also.

The earth, which had only heard such sounds as the humming of the winds and the dashing of ocean waves, now was full of sweet songs from the birds. It was full of beauty, as the bright-colored birds, like lovely jewels, flitted to and fro through the branches of the trees.

At last we come to the sixth day. On that day God made the animals of every kind and all creeping things.

Lions and tigers began to live in the deep woods where there had been no animals at all before. Great herds of cows and sheep fed in the wide meadows of the earth.

Goats and deer climbed the high mountains. Rabbits ran about in the grass and made their homes in the ground.

White bears tramped over the snow of the cold north. Hosts of chattering monkeys swung from the branches of the trees in hot countries. Soft purring kittens chased their tails and tumbled over each other in the grass.

Huge elephants and tall giraffes, big animals and small ones — God made all of them at this time.

"And God saw everything that He had made, and, behold, it was very good."

CHAPTER 3

The First Man, Adam

GENESIS 1, 2

There were now many animals, but there was not a man in all the wide world.

Last of all, God made a man.

God made the first man entirely grown up. It was a great deal better to make him grown up, because he was all alone in the world. If he had first been a little baby, he would not have been able to take care of himself.

God called this man "Adam."

God made man a body. He gave him eyes to see with, ears to hear with, a mouth to eat with, and feet to walk with.

But God made him different from an animal by giving this man a wonderful gift which animals did not receive.

Inside of man's body God put a living soul.

When you love your mother, is it her hands or feet that you love? No, it is something inside of your mother that you love, something that you cannot exactly see or touch. It is her soul that you love.

And it is your soul in you that loves your mother's soul. Your body cannot love or think.

You cannot see your soul, but it is there just the same, inside of your body.

Your body is the house of your soul.

Suppose that in an accident you should lose your arm. Would you be gone when your arm is gone? No, you would still be here. Suppose you were to lose your sight and become blind. Would you be gone if your sight were gone? No, though your sight would be gone, you would still be here.

Your arms and your eyes are parts of your body. They are not your soul. It is your soul that is *you.*

When God made man He gave him a wonderful soul which can love God and think about Him. An animal cannot think about God or love Him, because an animal has no soul. God created man in His own image. The Bible says, *"God formed man of the dust of the ground, and breathed into his nostrils the breath of life, and man became a living soul."*

This is the greatest gift that God could give to man, because the soul that God gave to man will never die.

When an animal dies, its body is dead, and that is the end of that animal. Its life is over, because it has only a body.

God did not give the angels bodies like ours. Angels are pure spirits, without bodies.

God also is a spirit without a body.

When the Bible says that God made man of the dust of the earth it does not mean that God picked up a handful of earth and made a man of it. It means that man's body is made of the same materials which we find in soil and rocks. When a man's body lies in the earth for a long time, it turns back to dust because it is made of dust.

But his soul does not die. When man dies, his soul returns to God who gave it to him.

God made both animals and man on that sixth day. And then He was finished with the making of earth and the heavens and all that is in them. *"And God saw everything that He had made, and behold, it was very good."*

On the seventh day God rested. He hallowed and blessed the seventh day, and rested from all His works that He had made. And He made that day a day of rest for man, too. On Sunday we rest from our daily work. Sunday is a day set apart for special worship of God with His people, a day to sing His praise together in church, to pray together, and to hear His Word.

CHAPTER 4

The First Woman, Eve

GENESIS 2

Do you think you would like to be Adam — all alone in the world? Adam was the only human being in the world. Yet he was not alone. God came to him and talked to him in the cool of the day.

But there was no other man, nor woman, nor child to whom Adam could talk.

At night he lay down on the cool grass to sleep. He had no house to live in, but he was not afraid, for none of the animals would hurt him. They were neither wild nor fierce.

God took care of Adam. God planted a most beautiful garden, and He filled it with beautiful trees and plants whose fruit was delicious to eat. He let Adam live in the garden and take care of it.

That beautiful garden was called the Garden of Eden, or Paradise. Every plant was pleasant to look at, and every fruit was good to eat in Paradise.

In the middle of the garden was a very wonderful tree called the Tree of Life. Whoever ate of that tree would live forever.

There was another wonderful tree that grew in the middle of the garden called the Tree of the Knowledge of Good and Evil.

God said Adam might not eat of the fruit of that tree, or he would die.

God had made Adam good. Adam was never naughty or wicked. He knew only about goodness; he did not know anything about badness. God did not want him to know anything about being wicked.

God warned him very plainly about the Tree of the Knowledge of Good and Evil when He commanded him not to eat of it.

Adam was very happy in the Garden of Eden. Once in a while he was lonely, because there were no other people in the world. He had neither wife, nor children, nor friends to talk to. But he loved the flowers and trees.

God brought all the animals to Adam so that he could name them and see if he could make a friend or companion of any of them. Adam gave names to all the animals. Each animal kept the name Adam gave it. But they could not understand his speech or talk to him.

Adam was still very lonely, and God said, *"It is not good that the man should be alone. I will make a help-meet for him."*

God caused Adam to fall into a deep sleep. When he was asleep God took out one of his ribs, and closed up the place from which He had taken it. God made that rib into a beautiful, sweet woman.

When Adam awoke, God brought the lovely woman to him.

How surprised and pleased Adam was! Now he was not alone any longer. Now he had some one to talk to and to love. Adam called her name Eve, and she was his wife. They could wander through the beautiful garden hand in hand, picking the good fruits to eat, taking care of God's garden together.

They did not have to wear clothes. They did not know anything about clothes. They went naked and were not ashamed, because they were innocent, as little babies. They did not yet know shame and sin. Their souls were white as snow.

CHAPTER 5

Adam and Eve Disobey God

GENESIS 3

Adam and Eve were happy. They were happier than anyone else has ever been in the whole wide world.

Why were they happier?

Adam and Eve were happier than anyone else has ever been because they were good in their hearts.

You know how happy you are when you are good·

Adam and Eve were always good. They loved God, they loved each other, and they never wanted to be naughty.

There is something in our hearts that wants to be naughty, because we have bad, sinful hearts. But when God made Adam and Eve, He gave them hearts that wanted to be good.

They were never sick. They were never very tired. When God made them He gave them bodies that were always perfectly well.

They never had to work hard, as we have to work now. All they had to do was to take care of the garden.

God also promised them a wonderful gift. He promised that if they obeyed His command not to eat of the fruit of that Tree of the Knowledge of Good and Evil, they would never die.

God made the first man and the first woman perfectly good, perfectly well. But think how much wickedness there now is in the world, and how much pain and suffering there now is, and worse than all — death! How has this sad change come about?

The wicked devil was once an angel in Heaven. But he did not stay good and pure, as the other angels are. He became wicked, and God turned him out of Heaven as punishment for his wickedness.

The devil, being very wicked, hated the good God, and tried to fight against Him.

When he saw the beautiful new world that God made, and Adam and his wife who loved God, the devil wanted to spoil God's beautiful world and make Adam and Eve bad like himself.

The devil knew that if Adam and Eve should become bad they could not live with God. He wanted them to be wicked and miserable.

So the devil, whose name is Satan, made use of a serpent, or snake. The snake was the wisest of all the animals which God had made. Satan, hiding himself in a snake, came and talked to Eve.

He asked, "Did God really say that you must not eat of any tree of the garden?"

Eve answered him, "We may eat of all the fruits of the garden, except of the fruit of the tree that is in the middle of the garden. God said that we must not eat the fruit of *that* tree, nor touch it, or we shall surely die."

Then the devil in the snake's body told Eve a wicked lie. He said to Eve, "No, you shall not surely die. God knows that when you eat the fruit of that tree your eyes shall be opened, and you shall be as God, knowing good and evil."

Eve was so foolish as to believe the snake instead of believing God. God had said that she would surely die if she ate of the fruit of that tree.

Eve went and looked at the tree. She thought the fruit might taste very good. It was a beautiful tree. She thought she would like to be wise, and to know evil as well as good.

She knew that God had commanded them not to eat of that tree, not even to touch it.

But Eve disobeyed God. She went up to the tree, picked some of the fruit, and ate it.

More than that she found her husband and told him what Satan had said. She picked some more fruit and gave it to her husband. He disobeyed God, too, and ate the fruit.

How wicked of them to disobey God, who had made them, loved them, and done so many wonderful things for them!

Now a horrible change came. No longer did they want to be good. No longer did they love God, and want to please Him! No longer did they love each other!

Now they had hateful, cross, and selfish feelings in their hearts. Now bad thoughts came into their minds. They began to want to do wrong things.

It was indeed true that the fruit of that tree would make them wise to know evil as well as good. Before this, they knew only what it was to have good thoughts and to be good. Now, at once, they knew what it was to have wicked thoughts, and to do wicked things.

Oh, how sad such knowledge was! How much better if they had known only the good!

It did not make them happy to know badness. It made them very unhappy.

Among other bad thoughts, they began to be ashamed that they were naked. Before this, they had never thought of being ashamed.

They took some big fig leaves and sewed them together — probably they pinned them together with little sticks — and in that way they made themselves aprons, so that they would not be naked.

CHAPTER 6

How God Punished Them

GENESIS 3

Adam and Eve no longer loved to have God come into the garden. They were afraid of God, because they knew that they had disobeyed Him. When they heard God walk in the garden in the cool of the day, they were afraid of Him and hid themselves among the trees.

Jehovah God called to the man and said, "Where are you?"

Adam answered, "I heard your voice in the garden, and I was afraid, because I was naked; and I hid myself."

Then God said, "Who told you that you were naked? Have you been eating of the fruit of the tree that I commanded you *not* to eat?"

And Adam, whose heart was now wicked, began to lay all the blame on his wife, although he was just as much to blame. He said to God, "The woman that you gave me to be with me, she gave me some of the fruit of the tree, and I ate it."

Then God said to the woman, "What is this that you have done?"

And Eve laid the blame on the snake.

She said, "The snake persuaded me, and so I ate the fruit."

Then Jehovah God said to the snake, "Because you have done this, you are cursed above all cattle, and above every beast of the field. You must crawl on your belly, and you shall eat dust all the days of your life.

"And I will put enmity between thee and the woman, and between thy seed and her seed: He shall bruise thy head, and thou shalt bruise his heel."

That curse, spoken by God so long ago, holds true even to this day. People all over the world hate snakes, are afraid of them, and try to kill them. Snakes hate men, and are afraid of them.

And since that time all snakes have had to crawl on the ground.

Then God gave a dreadful punishment to the woman who had so wickedly disobeyed His command. God told her He would punish her by giving her a great deal of sickness. She would have pain and weariness, and her husband would rule over her.

You see, it was Eve's disobedience that brought sickness and pain and weariness into the world. Eve would never again know what it was to be perfectly well. And when she should have any little children, they too would sometimes become sick and feel pain.

God told Adam that because he had listened to the voice of his wife, and eaten of the fruit of the tree that God commanded him not to touch, he too must be punished.

The ground would no longer grow fruits and vegetables by itself for Adam and Eve to eat. After this, Adam would have to work very, very hard to get enough to eat, until the sweat would pour down from his face.

Even when Adam should work hard to plant seeds, thorns and thistles would also come up, because God had cursed the ground as a punishment for his sin.

All his life Adam would have to work, and in the end he must die and his body must return to dust.

Oh, how wicked of Adam and Eve to disobey the command of the good God, who had made them good and very happy, and who had promised them everlasting life if they kept His one command!

What unhappiness they had brought upon themselves, and also upon all the people that would ever be born into the world! They no longer wanted to be good and to love God, or to love each other. Their hearts were full of badness now. They became selfish, untruthful, bad-tempered. Instead of loving to think about God, and to talk to Him, they wanted to forget about Him.

There was more sadness to come when God would send them little children. For the children would be like their father and mother; they would have wicked hearts, too.

That is why there is so much wickedness in the world. Just as black parents have black children only, and white parents have white children only, so parents having wicked hearts will have children with wicked hearts.

Adam and Eve were the parents from whom all the people in the world have come. If Adam and Eve had obeyed God, their hearts would have stayed clean and sinless, and all the people in the world would have had sinless hearts. But now we all are evil because Adam and Eve disobeyed God. The Bible says, *"There is none good, no, not one."*

Eve's disobedience brought sickness into the world, and now all of Eve's children must also know sickness and suffering, pain and weariness.

How hard men have to work to earn a living! Many poor people cannot earn enough to get proper food and clothing! This has come as the punishment for Adam's sin. If Adam and Eve had not sinned, no one would have to work so hard that work would become a burden.

And there is death. If there had not been any sin, we would have lived forever and ever. Perhaps we would not always have lived in this world. Perhaps God would have taken us up to Heaven to live with Him forever. But we would not have had to die first.

God is not only our Maker, but also our Ruler, and He will not allow anyone to disobey Him. Sin must be punished.

CHAPTER 7

A Loss and a Promise

GENESIS 3

Besides the Tree of the Knowledge of Good and Evil, there was another wonderful tree in the Garden of Eden. It was called the Tree of Life. Whoever ate of that tree would live forever.

Now that Adam and Eve had become wicked, God would no longer let them stay in the Garden of Eden for fear that they might eat of the Tree of Life, and live forever.

God drove Adam and Eve out of the Garden of Eden. To keep them from ever going back there, He placed Cherubim at the east of the garden to guard the way to the Tree of Life, and a flaming sword which turned every direction. Cherubim are heavenly beings, or angels, who stand by the Throne of God to serve Him.

When Adam and Eve were sent out of their home in the beautiful Garden of Eden, they had to make a home for themselves.

But things were not pleasant for them. Thorns and thistles began to grow. The trees were not full of delicious fruits for them to eat.

Adam had to work hard to get enough to eat, and Eve often felt tired and sick and unhappy. How they must have wished that they had not disobeyed God!

But now it was too late. They could not go back to the Garden, for at the entrance the Cherubim and the flaming sword guarded the way. They did not even dare come near the Cherubim, who had come down to earth to carry out the commands of God.

Was it altogether too late? Were Adam and Eve lost forever?

They could not go to Heaven with wicked hearts. Nor can we go to Heaven with wicked hearts. God is so pure and holy that He will not have the least bit of sinfulness in Heaven.

But, how can we go to Heaven, when our hearts are wicked? God, in His great love, has made a way.

For God loved man so much that He promised, way back in the Garden of Eden, that some day He would send His own Son into the world to become a man, to become one of Eve's children, and to die for the sin of the people.

And He kept that promise. He sent His own Son, Jesus, from Heaven. Jesus paid for sin. And if we believe in Him as our Savior and are sorry for our sins, He makes our hearts pure, and opens Heaven for us.

Wicked Satan wanted to have people sent to hell to be unhappy there with him. But God loved us so much that He gave His own Son to save us.

How we ought to thank Him!

God said, "Let there be light" and there was light. Genesis I

Cain did a dreadful thing. He killed his brother. Genesis 4

CHAPTER 8

The First Crime

GENESIS 4

Some time after Adam and Eve had been sent out of the Garden of Eden, something happened which showed that God still loved them.

God sent them a present—the first baby that ever was born in the whole wide world! How surprised and pleased they were! They had never seen anything like it before. But Eve knew that God had sent them their son.

A little while later, God sent them another baby.

They named the first baby Cain and the second one, Abel. And how they loved the two boys!

Cain and Abel did not have to go to school, because there were no schools and no books. There was a great deal to learn, however. They had to find out much by themselves, because they had no one except their father and mother to tell them how to do anything.

They had to learn which animals were safe to play with, and which were wild and dangerous. All the animals were not mild and gentle, as they had been before Adam and Eve sinned. Some of them were fierce and bad.

Cain liked to dig in the ground. He found out that by gathering seeds, by planting them in the ground, by watering them, and by digging out the weeds, he could make fruits and vegetables grow. He liked to do that; so he became a farmer.

Abel liked to play with the little lambs and goats. He learned how to lead them to the tenderest grass and the freshest water, and to drive away the fierce wolves and other animals which would have killed the sheep. So he became a shepherd.

But Cain and Abel had sinful hearts, like their father and mother.

When Adam and Eve saw their little boys doing naughty things, fighting and quarreling, they must have been more sorry than ever that they had brought sin into the world.

Of course, they taught their children about God. Abel learned to love God.

By and by, Cain and Abel grew up and became men. One day Cain brought a gift to the Lord. It was some of his fruits. Abel brought some of his little lambs to the Lord for an offering.

God was pleased with Abel's gift. He was not pleased with Cain's offering, because He saw that there was wickedness in Cain's heart. Cain did not feel sorry and ashamed because of his wickedness.

Cain became very angry that God was pleased with Abel's offering and not with his own. He fell into a dreadful temper. There was a black scowl on his face.

Cain knew that if he did what was right, God would be pleased with him. God told him that there was sin in his heart that made him do wrong.

But Cain was still very angry that Abel's gift should have been accepted, and his offering rejected. He was jealous of his brother, and he talked to Abel angrily.

One day, when he and Abel were in the field, he did a dreadful thing. He killed his brother!

Abel's blood ran out and soaked into the ground, making it red.

How sad Adam and Eve must have felt when they saw their son lying dead upon the ground. And to know that Cain had killed him!

Death must have seemed awful to Adam and Eve. They had seen dead animals, but no man had ever died before. Just a short time ago Abel had been full of life, talking and running and working. Now he lay there, white and still.

And they knew that it was their own sin which brought death into the world. They had eaten of the forbidden fruit. God had told them that death would come as punishment.

Oh, if only they had never disobeyed God!

Adam and Eve were not the only ones who saw Abel lying dead upon the ground, with his red blood staining the earth. God saw it, too!

God spoke to Cain. He asked, "Where is Abel, your brother?"

Cain told a wicked lie. He said, "I do not know. Am I my brother's keeper?"

God said, "The voice of your brother's blood is crying to me from the ground."

Then God gave Cain a dreadful punishment.

He said that the ground which had been soaked with his brother's blood would not grow things for him any longer. He must flee, and be a homeless wanderer on the earth.

So Cain went away to a far country and lived a lonely life, far away from his father and mother.

Cain took his wife with him when he left home. Adam and Eve must have had daughters, and Cain must have had one of them for his wife.

By and by, Cain and his wife had a baby, named Enoch. Enoch grew up and had a son, named Irad. Irad grew up and had children. And his children had children. After a while there was a son named Lamech, who had three sons. He named them Jabal, Jubal, and Tubal-Cain.

Probably all of Cain's children were evil like their father. But some of them were very clever.

Jabal was the first man to think of making a tent to live in. Jabal kept cows and sheep and goats, so that he would not have to go catch a wild one every time he wanted meat to eat or wool to make clothes of.

Jubal also was very clever. He was the first man to make a musical instrument. He found out how to make a whistle of a piece of wood. After making many whistles of different sounds, he put them together and made a kind of organ. Then, too, he found out how to fasten strings over a piece of wood so that they would make musical sounds like a harp.

Tubal-Cain found out something even more wonderful. He discovered how to make iron and copper red-hot until they were soft, as you have seen blacksmiths do, and how to beat them into shapes such as knives, swords, plows, and shoes. It was a great help to have good knives to cut with. Just think how hard it must have been to cut things with sharp stones or sticks!

When God made the world, He hid wonderful things in the earth for man to find and use. These three sons of Lamech quickly learned about some of them.

CHAPTER 9

What the First Men Were Like

GENESIS 5

I have been telling you all about wicked Cain and his descendants.

What are descendants? Children, and grand-children, and grand-children's children, and so on, these we call descendants.

How dreadful it would have been if all the people in the world had come from the wicked Cain!

God would not permit such a thing to happen, however.

God gave Adam and Eve another son to take the place of Abel whom Cain had killed.

Eve was very glad to have another baby. Cain had had to go far away, and she never saw him. Besides, he had caused them great sorrow. Abel was dead. Eve called this new son Seth. She said, "God has given me another son to take the place of Abel, whom Cain has killed."

Adam and Eve were a hundred and thirty years old when Seth was born.

Yet Adam was a very young man when he was a hundred and thirty years old. How is that possible?

God let Adam live a very, very long time. He was nine hundred and thirty years old before he died. He lived almost a thousand years!

Adam had a great many children, both boys and girls, before he died.

Most of Adam's children lived a long time, too. They also lived to be almost a thousand years old. Many of their children, in turn, lived almost a thousand years.

The world was becoming full of people. Many of those people lived to be almost a thousand years old.

The one who lived the longest was Methuselah. He lived to be nine hundred and sixty-nine years old. He was the oldest man that ever lived.

Why did God let those first people live so long?

The Bible does not tell us. But I shall tell you what I think. I think that they were very much stronger than people are now. God had wanted men to live forever. Even after they had sinned, and God had told them that they must die sometime, they still had a great deal of strength. They did not wear out as soon as we do.

The Bible tells us that many of them were giants — "mighty men of renown," the Bible calls them. They lived longer, and many of them were much taller and stronger than we are. Probably they had better minds than we have, too.

I think, too, that God let them live very long so that they should have time to learn how to do things, and then teach their children.

There was very much to learn. But God had made man with a desire to learn, and with a mind keen and bright to think and plan. So the people on earth soon learned how to build a house. They learned how to make axes for cutting down trees for lumber. They learned about fire—how to make a fire and how to use it for cooking food. They had to make kettles to hold the food they cooked, and they found copper and iron to use for that. How they must have enjoyed discovering new wonders every day! And they taught all these things to their children and grand-children.

Probably another reason the first people lived so long was so that they could teach their children and grand-children about God. Adam, who once had talked with God in the Garden, could tell them all about the wonderful first things.

For there was no Bible to read so that they might learn about God and His dear Son Jesus who was to come. After a while men learned to write. They learned to make the letters of the alphabet. But at first there were no books, and the only way things could be remembered was for fathers and mothers to tell their children all that they had learned from their parents and grand-parents.

Adam lived to tell the story of creation to very many children and grand-children and great-grand-children.

Among all those early people there was one man who did not live as long as the others. That man was Enoch. Enoch lived to be only three hundred sixty-five years old. And he did not die.

What happened to him then, if he did not die? Something very wonderful! Enoch was a very good man. He loved God and he prayed to Him. He thought about Him so much that it was just as if God were close to him, and he could walk and talk with Him.

The Bible says, "Enoch walked with God."

God loved this good man Enoch, and He did something very wonderful for him. God took him straight up to Heaven—took him up with his body, without his having to pass through the experience of death, as all other people must. The Bible says, "And Enoch walked with God, and he was not found, for God took him."

So you see, there was one man who was very good in that long, long ago. When we go to Heaven, we shall see that saintly man of old.

CHAPTER 10

The Second Beginning

GENESIS 6, 7, 8

PART 1 — BUILDING THE ARK

I am very sorry to say that although Enoch was a good man, many of the people were not good at all. They did not try to think about God. They tried to forget Him. When they forgot about God, they forgot to be good, also.

"And God saw that the wickedness of man was very great in the earth," and that man was thinking only of wickedness all the time.

Men were so bad that the whole earth was filled with violence. Murders, lying, stealing, fighting, and all kinds of wickedness were going on every day.

God felt sorry that He had ever made man on the earth.

"And Jehovah said, 'I will destroy man, whom I have created, from the face of the ground; both man and beast, and creeping things, and birds of the heavens.'"

God looked upon the earth, and He saw that the people had become very evil-minded. You would not like to have lived at that time, because you would have been afraid that some of the wicked people would hurt you or kill you. No one's life was safe. People had forgotten all about God.

But there was one good man in the world, and God did not want to destroy him. His name was Noah. He was the great-grandson of the good Enoch who went to Heaven without dying.

Although Noah lived among bad men all the time, he was a good man. He hated all the badness of the people around him.

He loved God, thought about Him, and prayed to Him. He would not do the wicked things that he saw the people around him doing all the time, or listen to their bad talk.

God spoke to the good man, Noah, telling him that he was going to destroy all the people in the world on account of their sins. When all the wicked people should be dead, Noah was to start a new world of people, because God had seen that he was a good man.

God told Noah to build a big ship, so that he and his sons and his wife and his sons' wives might be saved from the flood. They must bring into the ship with them two of every kind of animal — beasts, and birds, and creeping things — to keep them alive, and to start a new world after the flood.

Then God told Noah just how to make the ship, or ark.

He was to build it of very strong wood, and cover it inside and out with pitch to make it water-tight and to stop up all the cracks.

He was to make it very large, so that there would be room for all the animals.

It was to be four hundred fifty feet long. Now suppose you take a foot ruler and measure four hundred fifty feet on the sidewalk. Then you will see how very long the ark was. It was to be seventy-five feet wide. That is wider than most streets. It was to be forty-five feet high. That is as high as a high house. It was to have three stories in it. We might call them a downstairs, an upstairs, and an attic. There were to be rooms in it, probably so that Noah could keep the different kinds of animals separate, which otherwise would fight and kill each other.

There was to be a window in the ark, so that there would be plenty of air to breathe. There was also to be a door by which the animals and people could go in.

God told Noah to take a great deal of food into the ark, of all kinds that is eaten, so that he and all his family and all the animals might have enough food to eat when the flood came. For the flood was going to last a long time, and they would need a great deal of food when they were in the ark.

Noah began to build the ark, as God had commanded him.

It took him a very long time to build it. Perhaps it took him a hundred years. It had to be made very strong to keep out all the water, and very big to hold all the animals and the great amount of food they would need.

While Noah was busy with it, he preached to the people. He told them that God would punish them for all their wickedness, and that if they did not turn away from their sins, God would send a flood to drown them all. But they would not listen to Noah. They kept right on doing all the wicked things that they had been doing before.

They did not think that God would send a flood. They thought Noah was a very foolish man to go on building that big ship when there was no sign at all of any flood.

But Noah believed what God had said to him. He kept on building and preaching as he built.

At last, after a long time, the big ship was finished. Then Noah had to gather all kinds of food that is eaten by people and animals, and store it in the ark.

Then, when everything was ready, God told Noah to go into the ark with all his family, for in seven days He would send the rain. Two of every kind of animal must go in with them.

Noah went into the ark with his wife. His three sons, Shem, Ham, and Japheth, and their wives, went in also.

Then the animals began to come in. God must have made them willing to enter the ark, so that Noah would not have any trouble in leading them in.

Two and two—mates, a male and a female—every kind of animal, they came into the ark. Of some kinds of animals two had to go in, and of some seven.

How astonished the people round about must have been to see those animals marching into the ark in a long procession!

Here come the lions — the father lion and the mother lion — marching quietly along, and going right up into the ark.

Here are two tall giraffes, and here come two big gray elephants, and there come two tigers, with their beautiful striped coats. Two by two, they march into the ark.

Ah! here come the birds, flying two and two, straight into the ark.

Here come two big eagles; and there are two ravens. See them come — a perfect cloud of birds of all kinds! And here are two big ostriches, lumbering along, and two brilliant peacocks, with their tails outspread!

And here come creeping things — the snails, and hoptoads, and lizards.

At last the long procession came to an end, when two of every kind of animal that lived on the land were in the ark.

PART 2 — THE FLOOD

When they all were safe in the ark God shut the door. Then God sent the rain.

You have never seen it rain like that!

It did not come down in drops. It poured down! The Bible says, *"God opened the windows of heaven, and the fountains of the great deep were broken up."*

Soon all the land was covered with water. The terrible rain came down in torrents from the sky, and the great tidal waves rose up from the ocean and swept over the land with terrific force and swiftness, carrying everything before them, and covering the land many fathoms deep with water. All the wicked people were swept away with the force of the flood, and drowned.

The flood rose higher and higher. For forty days and nights — more than a whole month — the rain kept on pouring down in torrents. Tidal waves came up from the sea and swept over the land.

The waters bore up the ark, lifted it up above the earth, and floated it upon the waves.

"And the waters prevailed exceedingly upon the earth, and all the high hills that were under the whole heaven were covered." At last even the tops of the high mountains were covered, and the waters rose more than twenty feet above the tops of the highest mountains.

"And every living substance was destroyed which was upon the face of the ground, both man, and cattle, and the creeping things, and the fowl of the heavens; and they were destroyed from the earth: and Noah only, remained alive, and they that were with him in the ark."

The ark sailed upon the waters. When Noah and his family looked out of the window, they could see nothing but water — water, water, everywhere.

At last, after forty days and nights, the rain stopped.

For one hundred and fifty days the water covered the earth. Slowly it began to go down, but still no land could be seen. For five months, whenever the people looked out of the window, they could see nothing but water.

At the end of the five months, the ark, as it floated, struck something underneath. It was the high mountain called Ararat, and the ark rested upon the top of the mountain.

The waters kept on going down. After three months, upon looking out of the window, they could see the tops of the mountains.

After that Noah waited for forty days longer — more than a whole month. Then he opened the window, and he sent a bird called a raven out of the ark.

The raven, being a very strong bird, flew to and fro and did not come back to the ark.

At the same time, Noah sent out a dove to see if the waters had dried up from the earth.

But the little dove was not so strong as the raven, and she could not keep on flying all the time without any rest. She could not find any place that was not covered with water where she could rest. The dove flew back again, and Noah put out his hand and drew her into the ark.

Noah waited a week longer, and then he sent out the dove again. At evening she came back. In her beak she had an olive leaf that she had picked from some olive tree.

Then Noah knew that the waters were going away from the earth.

He waited a week longer, and then he again sent out the dove. This time she did not come back at all. So Noah knew that she must have found some dry place where she could stay.

When Noah was six hundred one years old, in the first day of the year, he took off the covering of the ark. He looked out and saw that the earth was dry.

He stayed two months longer in the ark, till the earth was thoroughly dry.

When Noah went into the ark, he was six hundred years and two months old. He stayed in the ark just one year and ten days.

PART 3 — GOD BLESSES NOAH

And God spoke to Noah, and told him to go out of the ark with all his family and all the animals. So Noah opened the door and stepped upon the solid earth of Mount Ararat.

Out flew the birds — so glad to be free!

Down the steep sides of the mountain ran the animals. They spread out in the woods and fields below, each kind of animal finding the sort of place it liked best. There it could make its home and have its little ones, and fill the earth again with animals.

The first thing that Noah and his family did, after they came out of the ark, was to kneel down and thank God for keeping them alive when all other men were drowned, and to promise Him that they would try to live so as to please Him. Noah took stones and made an altar. On the altar he burned animals as a gift to God. And God was pleased with Noah's gift.

So God blessed Noah and his sons, and told them to have a great many little children, to fill the earth with people again.

God gave them one command which they must obey. It was this: *"Thou shalt not kill."*

God promised to punish every man who kills another. He told Noah that if any man should kill another, the rest must punish him with death.

This is God's law, given long ago. Even to this day, over almost all the world, we still obey this law and put to death a murderer.

God also made a covenant with Noah and with all the animals that had been in the ark. A covenant is a solemn promise.

God's covenant was that He would never again send a flood to destroy all the people and animals in the world — never again as long as the world should stand.

God gave a sign to Noah, that He never would drown the world again. You have seen this sign many times, for God still remembers His promise. It is the beautiful rainbow!

Whenever you see the rainbow, remember that God has put it there because He wants you to remember His promise that He will never again destroy the whole world with a flood.

CHAPTER 11

The Strange Division of Men into Nations

GENESIS 10, 11

PART 1 — BEFORE THE DIVISION

Now after the flood Japheth and his wife made a home for themselves. By and by some little children were born to them: seven boys, and probably some girls.

When the children grew up, they also had children, and so on.

Shem and his wife lived in another place. They had five sons and some daughters. Their sons and daughters grew up and were married and had children.

Ham and his wife also had some children, four boys and some girls. They also grew up and had children.

By and by, the country began to be overspread with the children and grand-children of Shem and Ham and Japheth.

Each one kept apart from the others and lived in his own place.

From these three sons of Noah — Shem, Ham, and Japheth — all the people that now are in the world have come.

By and by there were so many people in the world that they began to build cities. In the course of time some of these cities became very large. The city of Nineveh was started at this time. Damascus, which is the oldest city in the world, was founded by Uz, the grandson of Shem. It still is large, for it has two hundred and fifty thousand people living in it today.

Noah, Shem, Ham, and Japheth, and their children and grandchildren lived very long lives, but they did not live quite as long as Adam and his children had lived.

Adam and his children and grand-children had lived almost a thousand years. Noah and his children lived to be six hundred years old. His grand-children lived to be five hundred years old.

After that, people lived to be four hundred years old, and then three hundred, and at last God cut down the life of man to one hundred fifty years.

In one respect, those early people were very much different from us. They all spoke the same language, and everybody understood everybody else.

Now some people speak English, and other people speak German. Some people speak French, and others speak Italian. The French cannot understand the Germans, the Germans cannot understand the English, and the English cannot understand the Italians.

But in those days, the Bible tells us, all the people spoke one language, and everyone understood everyone else. Not even the wisest man in the world knows what that first language was which Noah and his children spoke.

PART 2 — THE TOWER OF BABEL

As the number of the people increased, they moved farther and farther away from the mountains of Ararat. Gradually they began to spread far and wide over the earth.

As they traveled toward the south and east, they came to a plain in the land of Shinar. This plain was very well-watered, for it had the mighty river Tigris on the east, and the still greater river Euphrates on the west.

The people thought that this would be a good place to live. Here they built their homes.

In their pride they wanted to build a large city, with a tower so high that they could see it from a long distance. Then they could know in which direction the city was when they had traveled some distance away, and could easily find their way back. That, they thought, would keep them from separating and scattering over the whole earth.

A great many workmen came together to build the tower. They made bricks of mud and dried them in the sun. They built the tower of these bricks, using slime to hold them together. Slime is a kind of natural concrete which can be found on the ground in some parts of that country.

They all worked together busily. They shouted and called to one another.

One man might call, "Bring me some more bricks. I need some more for this corner."

Another would say, "I am ready for another pail of slime."

With all their bustle, it was a very noisy place. And as they kept on building, the tower became higher and higher.

The Lord came down to see the city. He saw that the people had begun to build the tower, and now they would stop at nothing that they might want to do.

God did not want them to stay in one city only, all huddled together. He wanted them to spread over the big world which He had made for man.

You remember that all the people spoke only one language.

But now God changed the speech of all the men without their knowing it, so that they did not understand each other. Each one spoke an entirely different language from that which he had spoken before.

When one man called out, "Bring me some more bricks," he was speaking in a new language that no one in all the world had ever heard.

The man he spoke to looked in astonishment at him, and asked, "What did you say?" But he also was speaking in a new language.

Although they tried again and again, neither of them could understand the other.

Then the first man called to another and said, "Here, something is the matter with this man. I have asked him ever so many times to bring me some more bricks, and he answers something that I cannot understand at all. Will you bring them to me, please?"

That man only stared at him.

"What did you say?" he asked, "I cannot understand you." But he also, without knowing it, was speaking another language that nobody had ever heard.

They shouted and called, and tried to make each other understand but it was no use. The louder they called, the less they understood each other. There was only a big noise and confusion.

They had to stop building the tower and the city. As they could not understand each other any longer, there was no use in trying to live together. So they all separated, and each went to live in a different place with his own family. They were scattered over the earth, just as God wanted them to be.

The name of the tower and of the city was "Babel." This means "Confusion," because there was a very big mix-up when God confused the language of the people.

Even to this day, when we hear a great confusion of noise, we call it a babel.

Look up on your map the Mountain of Ararat, the land of Shinar, and Babel.

CHAPTER 12

Abram Follows God

GENESIS 12, 13

PART 1 — ABRAM LEAVES HOME

After the flood people again increased in number. They were not as wicked as men had been before the flood. They were afraid, since they remembered very well how dreadfully God had punished wickedness.

Now God began to prepare the world for the coming of that Man whom He had promised. You remember that when God cursed the serpent for leading Eve into sin, He said that some day a child of Eve's would crush the head of the serpent.

Of course, the serpent really was Satan. When God promised that some day a child of Eve's should crush the serpent's head, He meant to say that some day a man would be born who would overcome Satan. Satan had caused sin and death to come into the world, but some day a man would be born who would again bring everlasting life by taking away the sin of the world.

He is Jesus Christ.

The first thing that God did to make the world ready for the coming of Jesus Christ was to pick out one good man, and to tell him to leave his country and his father's family, and to go to a country that God would show him.

That man was Abram. His wife's name was Sarai.

God said to Abram, "I will make of you a great nation . . . In you all the families of the earth shall be blessed."

God promised Abram that Jesus Christ would be one of his children's children or descendants. This was the son that had been promised to Eve, too. He, Jesus the Savior, was to take away the curse of sin and be a blessing to all the world.

Abram did as God had told him. He took his wife Sarai and his nephew Lot, whose father had died, and all the things that belonged to him, with all his servants, and left his own country of Haran to start on a long journey to a country far away.

Although Abram did not know where God wanted him to go, he obeyed God. He believed that God would take care of him.

It was a long journey to this far-away country. When Abram and Sarai said "Good-bye" to their relations and friends at Haran, it was for ever. They never saw any of them again.

Abram was not a young man when he left Haran. He was seventy-five years old. Sarai was almost as old, but men and women did not age as rapidly then as they do now.

Ladies, at that time, had nice things to wear, just as they do now. Sarai must have had beautiful golden bracelets for her arms, and golden anklets for her feet, golden earrings for her ears, and golden rings for her fingers. I am sure Sarai had a great many pretty clothes to wear. She was a very beautiful woman, and with her rich clothing and sparkling jewels, she must have looked very attractive indeed.

Although Abram and his household lived in tents, he was a very rich man. He had a great many cows, oxen, sheep, asses, and camels.

There were men-servants to take care of the animals. The women-servants milked the cows, made the cheese and butter, cooked meals for all of the large family, and wove the sheep's wool into cloth to be made into clothes.

Abram was so rich that he had more than three hundred men-servants, and probably as many women-servants. Of course, he could not manage his six hundred servants himself. Nor was he able to oversee his multitude of flocks and herds himself. He had an overseer, named Eliezer to do a great part of the managing.

At that time, of course, there were no railroads. Abram could not travel quickly to this far-away country. He had to travel by camel.

Sarai, Lot and his wife, and Eliezer rode on finely dressed camels.

The servants rode on asses, or walked.

Most of the servants were married, and there were many little children among them — even little babies. Of course, these little ones had to be carried in their mothers' arms, while the mothers rode on asses. Big baskets were flung across the backs of the asses, one on each side, and the children who were too young to walk were put into those baskets and carried in that way.

It seemed as if a whole village traveled along when Abram began his journey from Haran to this far-away country Canaan. Abram was a true chieftain — a man who had many servants, flocks, and herds.

Part 2 — Lot Chooses a Home

After a very long trip, Abram and all that belonged to him finally arrived in Canaan. This was the promised land — the country in which Abram was to stay for some time.

The servants drove the flocks and the herds along, so that they scattered over a large part of the country. There were no fences, and the animals could wander around, eating as they went.

Lot, too, had a great many flocks and herds and tents and servants.

Abram and Lot together had so many flocks and herds that the land could not take care of them. There was not enough grass for the animals to eat as they went along. As a result, Abram's servants and Lot's servants quarreled about the best pasture land.

Abram was too good a man to wish for any quarreling between his servants and Lot's.

He said to Lot, "Let us not quarrel, for we are relatives. It is better for us to separate, if there isn't enough grass in one place for both of us."

Abram was very generous. He let Lot have his choice of all the country round about.

Lot lifted up his eyes and looked over all the country. He saw, toward the east, the beautiful river Jordan. All the country near the Jordan was very green and beautiful, because it had many little streams and brooks running through it.

Lot chose that country. He thought he was choosing the best. But what a terrible mistake! For in that beautiful country were two of the most wicked cities that have ever been on this earth. Every day, Lot pitched his tents nearer to the wicked city of Sodom, and at last he reached the city and lived in it.

The Bible says that the men of Sodom were "wicked and sinners before the Lord, exceedingly."

What a dreadful place for Lot to live! How could his children grow up good?

But Abram kept on living in the land of Canaan in the Plain of Mamre.

CHAPTER 13

God Talks With Abram

GENESIS 13, 15, 16, 17

PART 1 — THE STORY OF A SLAVE

After Lot had separated from Abram, God came to Abram and told him to look as far as he could to the north, and to the south, and to the east, and to the west. All the land, as far as he could see, God promised to give to him and his children.

God also promised Abram that he should have many descendants, as many as the dust of the earth.

Although God made this promise, Abram had not even one little child at the time. He was no longer young, and you know people do not have children when they are old.

It must have seemed strange to Abram that God should promise that his children's children should be as many as the dust of the earth, when he did not have even one little child. But Abram knew that God is all-powerful, and Abram believed that God would do what He promised.

But at another time, when God made the same promise, Abram could not help saying, "But thou hast not given me any child at all."

Then God brought him out into the dark night, and told him to look up at the stars in the sky, and count them if he could.

God promised, "So shall thy descendants be."

Abram truly believed what God had said. That is what God wants us all to do: to believe what He has told us in the Bible. The Bible is God's book, and even if we give all our goods to feed the poor, if we do not believe what the Bible says, God will not be pleased with us.

It was because Abram believed God even when it was very hard to believe that God loved Abram very much.

God said that Abram's children should have all this land from the river of Egypt (that is the Nile) to the great river Euphrates.

Now Sarai, Abram's wife, felt very sorry that she did not have any children. Since she thought that she was too old to have a child, she said to Abram, "God has not given me any children, and perhaps you had better marry my maid Hagar. Perhaps God will give you and her a child."

Abram thought that Sarai's idea was a good one. Perhaps God would give him the long-promised child in that way. So Abram married Hagar.

But Sarai did not feel much pleased about it afterwards. For Hagar began to be rather rude to Sarai, and to feel that she was just as fine a lady as her mistress.

Sarai complained to Abram that Hagar was no longer behaving in a respectful way to her. Abram said to Sarai, "You may punish her, if she isn't respectful."

Sarai punished Hagar harshly, and Hagar ran away, far off into the desert.

The desert was not a very safe place for Hagar. There were wild animals there, and wild robbers too, sometimes. God was taking care of Hagar all the time, for He sent an angel down from Heaven to her. Hagar found a spring of water, and she sat down by it. Water is very important in a hot country.

The angel asked Hagar, "Where did you come from, Hagar? And where are you going?"

Hagar said, "I am running away from my mistress, Sarai."

The angel commanded her, "Go back to your mistress, and be obedient to her."

Then the angel promised Hagar that she would have a son. She was to name him Ishmael, because God had heard her trouble.

Now the name Ishmael means *God shall hear*. After Hagar had heard the words of the angel, she was very much comforted, because she knew that God was taking care of her. Then Hagar said, *"Thou God seest me."*

Hagar went back home. Before long a little son was born to her. He was Abram's son too. Abram named him Ishmael, as the angel had directed.

Abram was eighty-six years old when his son Ishmael was born.

Abram thought that God had given him the long-promised son. And Hagar was very happy with her little boy.

PART 2 — A PROMISE

God came and talked to Abram a great many times, so that Abram would not forget Him.

One day when Ishmael was thirteen years old, and Abram was ninety-nine, the Lord appeared again to Abram. Abram was now a very old man — too old to have children any more. His wife Sarai was ninety years old.

God said to Abram, "I am God Almighty. Walk before me, and be thou perfect."

Abram fell on his face, and while he was bowing low like that, God talked with him.

God said He would be with him, and he should be the father of many nations. His name should no longer be called *Abram*. It should now be *Abraham*. This name means *Father of many nations*. Sarai's name was changed to Sarah, which means *Princess*.

Then God said something to Abraham which greatly surprised him, for Abraham had thought that God had already given him the promised son when He gave him Ishmael. He did not expect another son.

Yet God promised him that the next year He would give Abraham and Sarah a son of their own.

Abraham was so much surprised that he laughed and asked, "Shall a child come to a man who is a hundred years old, and shall Sarah, who is ninety years old, have a child?"

God said, "Truly Sarah shall have a child, and you shall call him Isaac.

"I will bless Ishmael, too. He shall have twelve sons who shall become princes, and I will make of him a great nation too. Yet Isaac is the son with whom I will establish my covenant."

God repeated this promise to give Abraham and Sarah a son. One day Abraham was sitting at the door of his tent, resting himself. He lifted up his eyes and saw three persons standing near by.

Abraham knew at once that they were not men, but angels, and that one of them was God. He stood up quickly, went to them, and very politely bowed himself down to the ground.

He said, "My Lord, come and stay with me, I beg. And let a little water be brought in a basin to wash your feet."

In that very hot country, people wore only sandals on their feet, and their feet became very hot and dusty from walking on the burning sand. The first thing that any polite host would do was to wash the feet of his guests.

Abraham said to his visitors, "Come and rest yourselves under the shady tree. And I will bring a morsel of bread to refresh you after your journey."

The strangers answered, "Yes, do as you have said."

Abraham told a servant to take some water, and to wash their feet.

He himself hurried to Sarah's tent, and said, "We have some visitors. Quickly bake some nice cakes for them."

Then he ran to the herd of cows, and picked out a fine young calf. He gave it to one of his servants, and told him, "Kill it, cook it nicely, as quickly as you can, and bring it to me for the visitors."

After the meat was cooked and the cakes were baked, some servants brought them to Abraham under the tree. Abraham had brought milk and butter and he set all these things before his visitors, who ate them.

Now Sarah did not come out to see the visitors, because it was not considered well-mannered for women to come where men were.

Sarah could see them, however, as she stood in the tent door behind them, and she could hear what they said. She was listening closely, for strange visitors were not very common. And Sarah wondered who they were and what they had come for.

One of them asked, "Where is Sarah, your wife."

Abraham said, "In the tent."

God promised, "Next year I shall give Sarah, your wife, a son."

Sarah, in the tent door, heard it, and she began to laugh, saying to herself, "Shall I have such a pleasure as to have a baby, when I am so old? My husband is old, too."

She could not believe God's word, and she laughed.

The Lord asked Abraham, "Why did Sarah laugh? Is anything too hard for the Lord? Truly I shall give her a son next year."

Sarah came out of the tent, and said, "I did not laugh," for she was afraid.

The Lord said, "No, but you did laugh."

For God hears all that we say and knows all that we do.

CHAPTER 14

Sodom and Gomorrah

GENESIS 18, 19

PART 1 — ABRAHAM TRIES TO SAVE THEM

When the men were ready to leave, Abraham walked with them for a part of the way.

The Lord said He would not hide from Abraham what He was going to do. Because the sin of Sodom and Gomorrah was very great, He was going to those cities to see their great wickedness. So while the two angels went on toward Sodom, the Lord talked with Abraham.

When Abraham knew that God was going to Sodom and Gomorrah, he thought of his nephew Lot living in Sodom.

He drew near to the Lord, and asked, "Will God destroy the good people along with the wicked? There may be fifty righteous people within the city; will you not spare the city for their sakes?"

The Lord answered Abraham, "If I find fifty good people in Sodom, then I will spare the whole city for their sake."

Abraham was afraid to argue with God, but he knew there were not fifty good people in wicked Sodom.

He kept on, talking very humbly, "I who am but dust and ashes have taken upon me to speak to the Lord. It may be that there will be five less than fifty good people. Will God destroy all of the city for the lack of five people?"

The Lord said, "If I find forty-five good people I will not destroy it."

Abraham spoke once more, and said, "Perhaps there will be forty good people there."

And God said, "I will not destroy the city for the sake of the forty."

Abraham knew there were not likely to be forty good people in wicked Sodom, but he was afraid to keep on asking God, so he said, "Oh, let not the Lord be angry, if I speak once more. Perhaps there will be thirty found there."

And the Lord said, "I will not destroy the city for the sake of the thirty."

Because Abraham wanted very much to save Lot, he dared to speak once more, and entreated, "Behold, now, I have taken upon me to speak unto the Lord. Perhaps there will be twenty found there."

And the Lord said, "I will not destroy the city for the sake of the twenty."

At last Abraham said, "Let not the Lord be angry, I will speak only once more. Perhaps there will be ten found there."

And the Lord said, "I will not destroy the city for the sake of the ten."

Abraham thought that perhaps ten good people could be found in wicked Sodom.

These were Lot and his wife, and his two daughters who were married, and their husbands, and his two daughters who were not married, but this made only eight. Perhaps there might be two other good people in the whole city, Abraham thought, and that would make ten.

Just think what a wicked city it must have been, to have not even ten good people in the whole of it!

PART 2 — HOW THEY WERE DESTROYED

In the evening the two angels came to the city of Sodom.

Good Lot was sitting in the gate of the city. He saw the two angels and he stood up to meet them. He bowed with his face to the ground. This was the polite way to greet strangers at that time.

He said — for people were very hospitable in those days — 'My lords, come to my house to stay all night, and in the morning you may go on your journey."

At first they would not come in, but when Lot urged them very much, they at last entered his house.

Before bedtime, the wicked people of the city, both young and old, came from every part of the city, and gathered in a great crowd around the door of Lot's house. They called out to him, "Where are the men that came to your house tonight? Bring them out so that we can hurt them."

Lot opened the door of his house, went out to them, and shut it tightly behind him, so that the bad people could not get in, and he said to the wicked men, "I beg of you not to do such a wicked thing."

But the wicked people answered, "Stand back, or we will hurt you a great deal worse than we would hurt them." And they pushed Lot so hard that they almost broke down the door of his house.

These two men were not real men. They were angels and no one could hurt them. They put their hands out at the door, pulled Lot inside, and closed the door again. Then they caused all the bad people outside to become blind. Small and great alike, they fumbled and fumbled and could not find the door.

Then the angels told Lot that the Lord had sent them to destroy the city because it was most terribly wicked. He must get his daughters and sons-in-law who were living in the city and take them out of the place, for the angels would destroy the city.

But his sons-in-law would not pay any attention to Lot. They made fun of him. He could not do anything with them, and he had to go home without them or his daughters.

That night the angels stayed at Lot's house, but very early in the morning they awoke Lot, and said to him, "Get up, take your wife and your two daughters who are here, and hurry to get out of this city. Otherwise you too will be destroyed."

Because the angels did not think that Lot hurried fast enough, they took hold of the hands of Lot and his wife and his two daughters, and rushed them out of the city. Although God was going to destroy Sodom, He did not wish to destroy good Lot and his family.

When the angels had brought them outside of the city, they did not go any farther with them, but they said to Lot, "Escape for your life; look not behind you neither stay in the plain. Escape to the mountain, lest you be burned."

Lot begged to be allowed to go to a little city called Zoar, because he feared the mountain was too far away for him to be able to reach it safely.

The angel said that he might go to Zoar, since they would not destroy that little city.

Then the Lord sent upon those wicked cities of Sodom and Gomorrah one of the most terrible punishments that has ever come to pass.

God rained fire and brimstone straight out of Heaven upon those cities. They burned with terrible, roaring flames that reached up high into the air, so that all the sky was full of red hot flames and scorching cinders. All the houses and all the wicked people were burned to ashes. The roar of the flames could be heard for miles and miles.

Lot's wife, hearing the fearful noise and seeing the redness of the sky, disobeyed the angel's command not to look back. She turned around and looked at the fire. What happened? In one moment she was changed from a living woman into a pillar of salt.

Lot and his two daughters were saved. But after that awful fire, Lot was afraid to live in any city. He left the little town of Zoar to live in the mountain, where the angels had wished him to go. He and his two daughters had no house to live in. They had to live in a cave.

Oh, poor Lot! His home was burned; his flocks and his herds were destroyed; his wife was turned into a pillar of salt; and he and his two daughters lived in a bare cave. He was no longer a rich man. He had nothing at all now.

I am sure he now wished that he had not thought so much about the beautiful country, and about getting rich, but had thought more about serving God and about living with people who served Him too.

You cannot find Sodom and Gomorrah on your map, because they were destroyed. Nobody knows where they once were. But they were somewhere near the north end of the Dead Sea. You can find Zoar, however.

CHAPTER 15

Abraham Sends Ishmael Away

GENESIS 21

The next year God fulfilled his promise to Sarah that she should have a son. He sent her a dear little baby boy, and told her to call him Isaac.

Oh, how happy Sarah was that at last she had a baby of her very own! How happy Abraham was, too, that at last the long-promised child had come!

Abraham was one hundred years old at the baby's birth, and Sarah was ninety. God can do anything, and He gave them a baby by His almighty power in their old age.

His father being a very important man, Isaac was really a little prince. Abraham was very rich. He had more than three hundred men-servants who were born in his house, besides almost as many women-servants.

There was great rejoicing among all these servants when the little Prince Isaac was born.

When Isaac was about three years old, his father gave a fine feast or party for him. A great many people were invited. Even the servants came to the feast.

Little Isaac was dressed in his very finest clothes. Every one praised him, petted him, and made a great deal of him. He was a good little boy and everyone loved him.

There was one person who was not happy at the party. That person was Ishmael. Ishmael was a big boy now. He was fourteen years old. I am afraid he was jealous of all the attention that Isaac was getting. At any rate, he began to tease his little brother and to make fun of him.

When Isaac's mother saw and heard this, she was very angry to think that the son of the slave woman should mock her son Isaac.

She promptly went to Abraham, and said that he must send Hagar away with her son; for Ishmael, the son of a slave, teased and tormented Isaac.

This made Abraham feel very sad. Ishmael was his son, too. Of course he loved Ishmael, though he loved Isaac more.

In the meantime, God told Abraham not to be grieved because of what Sarah said, but to do what she wanted. God promised to take care of Ishmael because he was Abraham's son. He promised to make a great nation of him, too.

Abraham rose up early in the morning. He gave Hagar some bread, and a bottle of water to put on her shoulder. He kissed Ishmael, and sent both of them away into the desert.

The bottle was only an animal skin filled with water, but it was very important, since in that dry country it is often hard to find water. People die in the desert when they can find no water.

By and by, all the water in the bottle was used up, and Ishmael began to suffer from thirst.

He became too weak to walk any farther. His mother laid him down under the shade of a bush, and went a short distance away, beginning to cry. She thought Ishmael was going to die, and she could not bear to see him suffer.

Ishmael was crying, too, I think. Perhaps he was praying to God to take care of him, for his father had taught him to pray.

God was not going to let Ishmael die. No! God was going to take very good care of Ishmael, because he was Abraham's son.

God heard the voice of Ishmael.

The angel of God called to Hagar out of heaven, and told her not to be afraid that Ishmael would die, for God had heard Ishmael's voice. She must go and hold him in her arms. God was going to make a great nation of him.

God opened Hagar's eyes. What should she see but a fine well of water! Hagar went to the well and filled her bottle with water and took it back to Ishmael. She lifted up the poor weak boy and made him drink some water. Soon he felt much better and could run about as before.

After this, Ishmael always lived in the desert. He learned to shoot with a bow and arrow. When he wanted some meat, he could shoot a rabbit or perhaps a bird. The well gave him water to drink.

Although he lived in the desert, God took care of him.

When he was grown up, his mother took a wife out of Egypt for him. God gave him twelve fine sons. They lived in the desert of Arabia, and there the descendants of Ishmael live to this day.

They are called Arabs. They live in tents in the desert and travel about from one place to another on camels. They also have splendid horses. Arab horses are the finest in the world.

God kept His promise to Ishmael, for the Arabs are one of the great nations of the world today. There are many Arabs in the world now, and they are proud to count their descent from their first father, Abraham.

CHAPTER 16

Isaac, the Promised Son

GENESIS 22

Ishmael had gone away, and he never came back. He stayed in the desert, where God took care of him.

Isaac was the only son now. He was an obedient boy. His father and mother loved him very much.

His father taught him many things about God. He taught him to pray. Isaac paid attention to his father's teachings, and learned, while he was still young, to love God and to obey Him.

Abraham, his father, loved God very much. God loved him, too. God often spoke to him, and called him His friend.

Abraham loved his son Isaac almost too much.

God wished to see whether Abraham loved his son Isaac better than he loved God. He put Abraham to a very hard test.

God said to him, "Abraham!"

Abraham answered, "Here am I."

Then God said to him, "Take your son, Isaac, your only son, whom you love, and go to the land of Moriah. There I want you to build an altar and to offer up Isaac for a burnt offering upon one of the mountains which I will tell you of."

God knew this would be a very hard thing for Abraham to do, but he wanted to see if Abraham really loved Him enough to do it.

Long ago God had promised to send Isaac to Abraham, and to make him the father of many people.

How could this be, if Isaac had to be killed now? Abraham did not know, but he knew that God is all-powerful, and that He always keeps His promises. He knew that Isaac would be given back to him in some way. Perhaps God would raise him from the dead.

Abraham trusted God. Hard as it was, he was willing to obey.

He made wood ready to burn, and he took some fire, perhaps in a pan, since at that time they did not have matches.

Abraham rode on a donkey, because he was more than a hundred years old. The rest walked.

He took with him two strong young servants to carry the wood.

Since they had a long journey before them, they started very early in the morning. After they had traveled for three days, Abraham lifted up his eyes, and saw, far off, Mount Moriah, where God had told him to go.

He got down from the donkey and made a bundle of the wood. He tied it on Isaac's back so that it would be easy to carry. He took the fire in his hand, and a knife. Then he told the young men that he and the boy were going over to the mountain, and that they should stay where they were until he came back.

Abraham and Isaac walked along together. Abraham's heart must have been very sad, although he trusted in God.

He had not told Isaac what he was going to do. He could not bear to tell him.

After a while Isaac said, "Father!"

Abraham said, "Here I am, my son."

There was wickedness everywhere,
such wickedness as you can hardly imagine. Genesis 6

The name of the tower and of the city was Babel. Genesis 11

Abraham's servant gave Rebekah two beautiful gold bracelets. Genesis 24

That night a man came and wrestled with Jacob. Genesis 32

Isaac said, "Here are the fire and the wood, but where is the lamb for a burnt offering?"

Abraham said, "My son, God will provide Himself a lamb for a burnt offering."

They went on together until they came to the place that God had told Abraham about.

There Abraham built an altar. He laid the wood on the top, all ready to burn. Then he took his dear son and tied him so that he could not get away, and he laid him upon the altar.

He must have told Isaac what he was going to do, and he also must have told him that he believed that God would raise him from the dead. Isaac was big and strong enough to struggle so that Abraham could not have bound him against his will. But he, too, knew that he must obey God, and he must have trusted that God would take care of him.

At last Abraham reached for the knife to kill his son. Just as he was going to strike Isaac, he heard someone call, "Abraham, Abraham!"

He stopped in surprise and looked around to see where the voice came from. He answered, "Here am I."

Then Abraham knew that it was the angel of the Lord calling to him.

The voice said, "Lay not your hand upon the lad, and do him no harm. Now I know that you fear God, seeing you have not withheld your son, your only son, from Me."

Oh, how happy Abraham felt now! His boy had been given back to him, almost from the grave! He was happy, too, because he had done what God commanded him, and he felt that God loved him. It always makes us happy when we obey God. And Isaac felt happy, too, you may be sure.

Abraham untied Isaac. In a few minutes, as he was looking around, he saw a ram which was caught in a thicket by its horns. Abraham took the ram and offered it for a burnt offering instead of his son Isaac.

Soon the angel of the Lord called to Abraham out of heaven a second time.

God made an oath, the strongest and most solemn promise that one can make. The Lord promised that because Abraham had been willing to sacrifice his only son, He would give him the greatest of blessings. He would make his descendants as many as the stars of the heaven, and as the sand of the seashore. They should overcome their enemies, and in them should all the nations of the earth be blessed.

When you go to bed tonight, look up at the stars. Can you count them? Of course you cannot. But the people who have come from Abraham are just as many as the stars. Can you count the grains of sand in a single handful? Think of how many grains there must be in all the sand of the seashore! Then remember God's promise to Abraham.

God had repeated this promise to Abraham five times. He has fulfilled that promise. God rewarded Abraham wonderfully for that act of obedience in offering his only son to God. The Jews are Abraham's children. Many of the races which lived during the time of Abraham have entirely died out, so that there is not one man left today. But there are millions of Jews in the world today.

When God said that all the people of the world should be blessed in Abraham, God meant that one day our blessed Savior, Jesus Christ, would come into the world to save the world from sin, and to bring everlasting life. Jesus would be born a long time after Abraham, but He would be one of Abraham's descendants.

CHAPTER 17

Rebekah

GENESIS 24

PART 1 — AN ANSWER TO A PRAYER

After Isaac had grown up, his mother Sarah died. Abraham did not have any place in which to bury her. Although God had often promised that the whole land of Canaan would belong to his family at some future time, he did not now own any of it. He lived in tents and wandered from one place to another.

Abraham went to the people of the country of Canaan, saying to them, "I am a stranger among you, and I do not own any land. Be so kind as to let me buy a piece of land, so that I may have a place to use as a burying-ground."

The people were very kind, and after a good deal of politeness on both sides, they sold Abraham a field that had a cave in it, called the Cave of Machpelah. Here he buried his wife Sarah.

After Sarah died, Abraham and Isaac were lonely. Abraham was a very old man. Isaac was forty years old, but he was not yet married. Abraham did not want him to marry any of the heathen women who lived near them. Before he died, Abraham wanted to see Isaac married to a good woman, one who worshipped God and not heathen idols.

Abraham called his oldest servant, his steward who ruled over all that he had. Abraham made him make a very solemn promise that he would not take a wife for Isaac from the Canaanite people living in the neighborhood.

Abraham made his old servant promise to go back to the country where Abraham had come from, and get a wife for Isaac from some of Abraham's relatives.

The servant started on his long journey through the hot sandy country. He took ten camels with him. He took servants also, for safety's sake. In that time, and in that lonely country, it would not have been safe for one man to travel alone, even on a swift-footed camel. Besides, he hoped to bring some ladies back with him.

At last, after several days of travel, he reached the country that Abraham had come from, and the city where Abraham's brother Nahor lived. This city was named Haran.

Outside the city was a well of water. In that dry country there was often only one well for a whole city. Every night the young girls of the city went out to the well, with tall pitchers balanced on their heads. They let down their pitchers into the well and drew water. Then they carried it home on their heads for the family to use.

When Abraham's servant came to Haran, he made his camels kneel down by the well. It was evening — just the time when the young girls always gathered around the well to draw water.

Abraham's servant was a good man, who believed in God. He had come safely on his journey and had reached the city to which Abraham had sent him. But he thought to himself, "How shall I be able to tell which young girl is the one that God wants Isaac to have for his wife?"

He kneeled down on the ground beside the well and bowed his head. He prayed, saying "O Lord God of my master Abraham, help me this day! When the daughters of the people of the city come down to draw water, and I say to one of them, 'Let down thy pitcher, I pray thee, that I may drink,' and she shall say, 'Drink, and I will give thy camels drink also,' let that be the one whom Thou hast appointed as a wife for Isaac."

God often answers prayer almost before we have asked, and He did so this time. Before the servant had finished praying, a very beautiful girl named Rebekah came to the well.

The servant thought, "Can this be the right one?" He ran to her and said, "Let me, I pray thee, drink a little water out of thy pitcher."

The girl said very politely, "Drink, my lord, and I will draw water for thy camels also till they have finished drinking."

She said just the very words that the servant had prayed to the Lord that she should say!

She took down the pitcher from her head, and let him drink. Then she emptied the rest of the water into the drinking trough for the camels. She filled the trough till all the camels had had a drink.

The servant was very much astonished to have her say and do just as he had prayed that she might. Had his prayer been answered so soon?

When the camels had had enough water, he gave her a rich golden ring which he had brought with him, and he put on her arms two beautiful golden bracelets.

Then he asked her, "Whose daughter are you? Is there room in your father's house for us to lodge?"

She answered, "I am Nahor's grand-daughter. We have plenty of room for you to stay with us, and straw and food for the camels."

Nahor, you know, was Abraham's brother.

When the servant heard this, he was so happy that he bowed down his head to the ground and worshipped, saying, "Blessed be the Lord God of my master Abraham, who has led me to the house of my master's family."

PART 2 — THE SERVANT'S STORY

Now Rebekah had a brother named Laban. Rebekah told him all that the man had said to her. When Laban heard this, and saw the rich jewels that the man had given her, he went as quickly as he could to the well. He said at once, "Come, you are blessed of the Lord. Why do you stand here? The house is all ready for you, and there is plenty of room for your camels."

The servant entered the house. Laban unharnessed the camels and gave them food and bedding. Then he brought water to wash the feet of the servant and of the men who had come with him.

All the people in the house were glad to see the servant of Abraham.

They knew he must be tired and hungry after his long journey, and so they made supper ready for him.

But he said to them, "Before I eat supper, I must tell you what I have come for."

They were eager to listen. In those days there was no mail to bring letters. People never heard about their friends who had gone away, unless some traveler brought news from them. Probably Abraham's relatives had not heard anything about him since he left home sixty years before.

They gathered around the servant to listen to the news he brought of their Uncle Abraham.

He began his story, "I am Abraham's servant. The Lord has blessed my master Abraham greatly. He is very rich, for God has given him flocks, herds, camels, asses, silver, gold, men-servants, and maidservants.

"In his old age, God gave him one son, Isaac. Isaac will be very rich, too, because Abraham has given everything that he has to his son.

"My master does not wish his son to marry a wife of the heathen Canaanites of the land where he lives, and he made me swear a solemn oath to go to his father's country, to his own family, and to get a wife for his son from among them.

"And I said to my master, 'Perhaps the woman will not be willing to come with me.'

"And my master said to me, 'The Lord, whom I serve, will send His angel with you to prosper your way. You must go to my own family and take one of the women to be a wife for my son.'

"I came this day to the well, and said, 'O Lord God of my master Abraham, behold, I stand by the well of water. When a young girl comes to draw water, and I say to her, Give me, I pray thee, a little water to drink, and then she shall answer, Drink, and I will also draw water for your camels — then, O Lord, let that be the woman whom the Lord has appointed for my master's son.'

"Before I had finished my silent prayer, I saw Rebekah coming, with her pitcher on her shoulder. She went down to the well and drew water.

"I said to her, 'Let me drink, I pray thee.'

"And she made haste and let down her pitcher from her shoulder, and said, 'Drink, and I will give thy camels to drink also.'

"I asked her, 'Whose daughter are you?' And she said, 'I am the grand-daughter of Nahor.' "

While the servant was speaking, they were gathered around him, listening most eagerly to all that he said. They were astonished to see how wonderfully God had made everything happen just as the servant had prayed it might. They, too, were worshippers of God.

The servant went on. "I gave her the golden ring, and put the bracelets on her arms. Then I bowed my head and worshipped the Lord of my master Abraham, who had led me in the right way to take my master's brother's daughter to be the wife of his son Isaac."

At last the servant asked, "I want you to tell me whether you will let Rebekah go back with me to be my master's son's wife?"

Nahor's family felt that it was truly by God's guidance that all these things had happened.

They said, "This is truly God's doing, and we must not hinder it. Behold, here is Rebekah. Take her, and go, and let her be thy master's son's wife, as the Lord has spoken."

When Abraham's servant heard that they were willing to let her go, he felt still more grateful to God. He bowed himself down to the earth, and thanked the Lord for helping him in this wonderful way.

Then he opened the packs on the backs of the camels. He brought out some beautiful jewels of gold, some jewels of silver, and some very rich and handsome silk clothes. He gave these to Rebekah. He also gave some precious presents to her mother and her brother.

PART 3 — THE END OF THE JOURNEY

In the morning the servant said, "Now I must return to my master."

Rebekah's mother and brother said, "Oh, do not be in such a hurry. Let her stay with us at least ten days."

He said, "Do not hinder me. Let me go back to my master."

"Well," they said, "we will call Rebekah and see what she says."

They called her and asked her, "Are you willing to go with this man right away?"

"Yes," she said, "I will go."

They let Rebekah go. They bade her good-bye very affectionately, and blessed her.

She did not go alone to her new home. She took her old nurse as maid, and some girl friends as companions. Then she would not become homesick far away in a strange land.

They all rode upon the camels that Abraham's servant had brought.

Abraham himself, as you know, was a worshipper of God and had taught his son to worship God also. Isaac was a very good man. One evening he took a walk in the fields so that he could quietly think about God and pray to Him.

Looking up, he saw a cloud of dust in the distance. Very soon he saw that it was the camel train coming back.

Rebekah also saw Isaac walking in the fields, and she said to the servant, "What man is this walking in the field to meet us?"

The servant said, "It is my master."

Rebekah made her camel kneel down so that she could get off. She wanted to dress herself properly before she met the man who was to be her husband.

In that country young ladies always had their faces covered with veils. It was not considered proper for a lady to appear without her veil. Rebekah hastened to wrap herself from head to foot in a long veil. Only her beautiful eyes could be seen.

She was ready now to meet her future husband. In a few minutes the camels approached Isaac. When he saw the beautiful young girl whom the servant had brought with him, he fell in love with her. He brought her home with him, and took her into the tent which had been his mother's. Soon they were married.

And Isaac felt comforted after the death of his mother Sarah.

The time finally came when Abraham, too, must die. He had had a long life of one hundred seventy-five years.

His sons, Isaac and Ishmael, buried him in the Cave of Machpelah, where Abraham had buried his wife Sarah, after buying the field from the people of the land for a family burial-place.

Abraham was one of the best men that has ever lived in this world, although he lived before the Bible was written, and in a country of heathen idol-worshippers. He was called the friend of God. He obeyed God in everything, just as a little child obeys its father. God loved him and talked to him.

Because Abraham trusted God so simply, and obeyed Him so well, God made him the father of the great nation of the Jews. From his descendants later came Jesus.

Abraham is in Heaven now, and if we love God and try to please Him, we shall one day see Abraham in Heaven.

CHAPTER 18

Jacob Buys the Birthright

GENESIS 25

Isaac was forty years old when he married Rebekah. For twenty long years they had no little children to brighten their home.

This was a great disappointment to them; so Isaac prayed to God and asked Him to give them a child.

God heard Isaac's prayer, for He is a prayer-hearing and prayer-answering God. He gave them more than they had asked for — he gave them twin baby boys.

They named the first one Esau, which means *red*. When he was born he was covered with soft red hair. The second one they called Jacob.

Although these boys were twins, they were not one bit alike. Esau had red hair and a very hairy skin, but Jacob had a soft, smooth skin. Nor were they alike in character. Esau was an outdoor kind of boy who loved sports; but Jacob was a home-loving boy who loved to stay in the tent with his mother.

Esau hunted wild animals and shot them with his bow and arrow, bringing them home for the family to eat.

Isaac was very fond of the tasty meat which Esau prepared for him. He praised Esau more than Jacob, but Rebekah loved Jacob best.

One day Esau was out hunting in the fields, and Jacob was at home cooking some delicious vegetable soup. Esau came home tired out, and so hungry that he felt as if he would die of hunger. When he came unto the tent, he smelled that delicious soup.

He said to Jacob, "Give me some of that good soup that you are cooking, for I am almost dying of hunger."

Now Jacob might have been generous enough to give his hungry brother some of his soup, but Esau had something that Jacob wanted just as much as Esau wanted the soup. Jacob thought that if Esau wanted the soup very much, this would be a good chance for him to offer the bargain. Jacob wanted Esau's birthright.

I shall explain to you what a birthright is.

It is the right which belongs to the oldest son in a family to have a larger share of his father's possessions when the father dies, than any of the other sons.

In this country we do not have such a thing. Each son is usually treated like the others. In some countries the oldest son is often favored even today.

Even though these two boys were twins, Esau was a little the older, and so the birthright belonged to him. Jacob must have often felt that, since there was so little difference in their ages, it was unfair that Esau should have the birthright and all it meant. Jacob was jealous of Esau.

There was another reason why Jacob thought the birthright might better be his than Esau's. Esau, from the time that he was a little child, had been a careless, thoughtless boy. He paid very little attention to serious things. But Jacob was a thoughtful boy. He listened attentively when his father Isaac talked to him about God.

Abraham, too, had told the two boys about God. They were fifteen years old when grandfather Abraham died, and he had often told them his wonderful story — how God commanded him to leave his family and his country, and go to a strange country that he did not know; how God told him that all this country should belong to his children's children; how his children should be as many as the stars, and the sands of the seashore.

Esau had paid very little attention to the things that grandfather was saying. He did not think them very interesting. He would rather be off hunting than listen to grandfather's stories.

But in Jacob's heart these stories sank down deep — how God commanded Abraham to sacrifice his son Isaac, and how God sent an angel to rescue Isaac. Time and again Jacob heard Abraham tell of God's promise that in his family all the earth should be blessed.

And Jacob thought it a pity that such a wonderful birthright belonged to Esau, who was so indifferent. Esau did not seem to care. Many times Jacob wondered if he could not somehow take away that birthright from him.

Now he saw his chance. Esau came home from the hunt and wanted soup.

Jacob said to Esau, "I will give you some of my soup, if you will sell your birthright to me."

You would expect Esau to say, "What? Sell you my birthright for a little bit of soup? No, indeed!"

What he really did say was, "Here I am ready to die of hunger. What good will this birthright be to me? You may have it, if you will give me some soup."

Jacob thought, "When Esau gets over being hungry, he will be angry and refuse to keep to the bargain."

So he said, "First promise that you will really give me the birthright."

Esau impatiently promised, and reached for the dish.

So Jacob bought the birthright which Esau valued so little.

CHAPTER 19

Jacob Deceives His Father

GENESIS 27

PART 1 — REBEKAH'S PLAN

Isaac, as you remember, was forty years old when he married Rebekah, and he was sixty years old before Jacob and Esau were born.

His sons had now grown to be men, forty years old, and Isaac was a hundred years old. His eyes were dim, so that he was almost blind.

He was a good man who worshipped and loved God. God had appeared to him once and had blessed him, giving him the same promise that He had given to his father, Abraham.

Isaac had inherited great riches from his father, and he became still richer. He had "possessions of flocks, and possessions of herds, and a great store of servants." He was a great and mighty prince in the country.

His son Esau gave him a good deal of worry. First he sold the birthright. Then he went out and visited the heathen Hittites who lived nearby. After a while, he even married two Hittite wives. This was wrong. If he had children, his wives would be sure to bring them up to be heathen, and to worship heathen idols. Esau had not paid much attention to the teaching of his grandfather, Abraham, or he would have known that God wanted his family to keep apart from the heathen.

Isaac, being now a hundred years old and nearly blind, thought that it was almost time for him to die.

One day he called his older son, Esau, to him. He said, "Behold I am old, and I know not the day of my death.

"Now I want you to do something for me. I want you to go hunting and get me some meat and cook it the way I like it. Then bring it to me to eat and I shall give you my blessing, before I die."

Esau had sold his birthright to Jacob for "a mess of pottage," which was some soup. After the soup was eaten, he had begun to wish that he had not been so foolish and hasty as to sell his birthright. Now he thought that perhaps his father would give him back part of the birthright when he blessed him.

Perhaps his father intended to do that, for he loved Esau best. Yet it was all going to turn out very differently from what they expected.

Rebekah overheard Isaac speak to Esau. She loved Jacob more than Esau, and she wanted him to have the blessing instead of Esau.

She called Jacob and told him what she had heard his father say to Esau.

"Now, therefore, my son," she said, "obey my voice and do what I command you.

"Go to the flock and fetch me two good kids of the goats. I shall cook them and make them savory meat, just as your father loves it. You must take it in to him. He will give the blessing to you, instead of to Esau, if you bring him the meat."

Jacob answered, "My father is blind and cannot see, but perhaps he will touch me. I have a smooth skin, and Esau is hairy. Father will know that I am not Esau when he touches my skin.

"And if Father finds out that I am deceiving him, he will be angry, and he will curse me instead of blessing me."

His mother said, "If he curses you, I will bear the curse instead of you. Only go and do what I have commanded you."

Jacob brought the kids, and his mother cooked them just as his father liked to have meat cooked.

Then Rebekah took one of Esau's best garments and told Jacob to wear it. She fastened some pieces of the kids' hairy skin on his hands and on his smooth neck so that Jacob might deceive his blind father.

So Jacob went in to his father and said, "My father."

PART 2 — THE BLESSINGS

Isaac answered, "Here I am. Who are you, my son?"

Jacob answered, "I am your older son, Esau. I have done what you told me to do. Now come and eat of the meat, so that you may bless me."

Isaac asked in surprise, "How is it that you found it so quickly?"

Jacob said, "Because the Lord, your God, brought it to me." (How he dared to tell this wicked lie, I cannot understand.)

Isaac was not quite satisfied. He was a little suspicious. It did not seem to him that the voice sounded like Esau's. He said, "Come here, so that I may touch you and see if you are truly my son Esau."

Jacob came near, and his father felt his hands, now covered with the hairy kidskin. He said, "The voice is Jacob's, but the hands are the hands of Esau."

To settle it, he finally asked, "Are you truly my son Esau?"

And Jacob answered, "I am."

Isaac said, "Bring the meat to me. I shall eat of your meat, so that I may bless you."

Jacob brought the delicious food to his father. He brought him some wine. Poor blind Isaac ate and drank, thinking Esau was with him.

After he had finished, he said, "Come near, and kiss me, my son."

Jacob did so.

His father smelled the smell of Esau's garment, and he said, "See, the smell of my son is as the smell of a field which Jehovah has blessed.

"And God give thee of the dew of heaven, and of the fatness of the earth, and plenty of grain and new wine.

"Let peoples serve thee, and nations bow down to thee.

"Be lord over thy brethren, and let thy mother's sons bow down to thee; cursed be every one that curseth thee; and blessed be he that blesseth thee."

Now it happened as soon as Isaac had finished blessing Jacob, when Jacob had gone out from the presence of Isaac, that his brother Esau came in from his hunting.

He had savory meat prepared, and he brought it to his father.

He said to him, "Let my father now arise, and eat of my meat, that thy soul may bless me."

How startled poor Isaac was! He cried out, "Who are you, then?"

Esau said, "I am Esau, your son, your first-born."

Then Isaac trembled and said, "Who was it then that brought meat to me? And I ate it before you came, and I gave him the blessing. The blessing is his now. I cannot take it back!"

Esau broke into a bitter cry. "Oh, my father, bless me also, even me also!"

Isaac said, "Your brother came and deceived me, and he has taken away your blessing."

Esau cried out, "He has done this twice. He took away my birthright, and now he has taken away my blessing." Again he asked bitterly, "Have you not saved a blessing for me, my father?"

Isaac said, "I have made him lord over you, and I have given all his brothers to him for servants.   I have promised him corn and wine. What more can I give you, my son?"

Poor Esau cried, "Have you only one blessing? Bless me, even me also, O my father!"

Then his father gave him a blessing, too, but he could not give him as good a promise as he had given Jacob.

He said to him, "Behold, of the fatness of the earth shall be thy dwelling, and of the dew of heaven from above. By thy sword shalt thou live, and thou shalt serve thy brother; and it shall come to pass when thou shalt break loose, that thou shalt shake his yoke from off thy neck."

These blessings that Isaac gave to his two sons were not only for Jacob and Esau. They were meant also for their descendants. They foretold what would happen to the children of Jacob and Esau and their families, long after they themselves were dead. That was what made the blessings of very great importance·

Although Isaac had intended to give the best blessing to Esau, and although Jacob had been wrong to deceive his old father and to cheat his brother out of his birthright, yet God was ruling all this. It was God's will that Jacob should be the one who should have both the birthright and the best blessing. Jacob afterwards became a very strong and good man, but Esau was always a weak man.

CHAPTER 20

Jacob Leaves Home

GENESIS 27, 28

PART 1 — A HURRIED FLIGHT

After the blessing had been given to Jacob, Esau hated Jacob for cheating him. He said in his heart, "My father is an old man. Very soon he will die. Then I will kill my brother."

Someone, probably one of the servants, hearing Esau threaten thus, told Rebekah.

Jacob had done a very wicked thing in deceiving his old, blind father by telling lies, but his mother was as much to blame as he was. Rebekah must have seen that weak, impulsive Esau was not a fit person to receive the birthright and the blessing; that he was not fit to carry on the honor of the family, and to be the kind of man that God wanted Abraham's grandson to be.

At the same time, Rebekah did not do right in deceiving Isaac. We must never do wrong, even to make right come out of the wrong. If Rebekah could not manage in an honest way that Jacob should have the birthright and the blessing, she should have left it to God.

Of course, Rebekah was now in great fear for the safety of Jacob. To save Jacob's life, she planned to send him away from home for a while until Esau should get over the fierceness of his anger.

She said to Jacob, "My son, Esau is so angry with you that he will kill you when your father dies. The best thing for you to do is to flee away to my brother Laban in Haran. Stay there a few days, till your brother's fury is turned away, and he has forgotten what you have done to him."

They both knew that Esau was not a very strong character and that, though he was very angry now, he would soon forget his anger.

Rebekah did not tell Isaac that she wanted to send Jacob away for safety's sake. She gave another reason. She said to him, "Jacob must not marry one of the heathen Hittites who live around here."

Isaac agreed with Rebekah.

He called Jacob and said to him, "We do not want you to take a heathen wife as Esau has. Now, you go to Padan-Aram, where your mother came from, and take a wife from one of the daughters of your mother's brother Laban."

They did not give Jacob servants and camels to go with him, as Abraham had done when he sent his servant to bring a wife for Isaac. They let him go all alone and on foot. His father was a very rich man; he could easily have given his son both servants and camels. Perhaps Rebekah had to send Jacob off quietly and quickly, for fear that Esau would follow him and kill him.

His mother told him before he started that when Esau's anger cooled down, she would send for him to come back.

She could not keep that promise. Jacob did come back, but not till his mother had died. When Jacob said "good-bye" to her, it was forever. They never saw each other again. That must have been God's punishment to them.

His father Isaac blessed him and said to him, "May God Almighty bless thee, and give thee the blessing of Abraham, that thou mayest inherit the land wherein thou art a stranger."

So Jacob said "good-bye" to his dear father and mother, and started out on his long and lonely journey. It was more than three hundred miles to Haran, where Jacob's uncle Laban lived. Many days he had to tramp over the hot and burning sands, and many a night he had to lie down on the bare ground and sleep under the open sky

After Jacob had traveled for a few days over the lonely country, he became very tired. Lying down at night on the hard ground under the stars, he felt lonesome and unhappy. He knew that he had done wrong to deceive his old, blind father, and to steal his brother's blessing. He knew that Esau was very angry with him and would kill him if he could.

All these thoughts made Jacob unhappy. He was worried, too. He was afraid that he could not make that long journey safely on foot. There were wild animals in that country. It was hard to get enough to eat. Sometimes he was very hungry.

But Jacob was not really alone. God had been with him all the time.

God was taking care of Jacob, although he did not deserve God's care.

PART 2 — JACOB'S DREAM

One night Jacob felt so tired and weak that he thought he was going to die, all alone in a strange country. He had walked all day. His feet were sore, and he was faint. He took a stone for his pillow. Then he lay down in that place to sleep.

While he was asleep, he forgot all about being tired and lonely, for he dreamed a most wonderful dream.

He saw a ladder, so long that it seemed to stand upon the earth and reach to Heaven. On the ladder he saw bright angels walking up and down. This beautiful sight filled Jacob's mind with wonder. At the top of the ladder stood the Lord.

The Lord spoke to Jacob: "I am Jehovah, the God of Abraham, and the God of Isaac, your father. The land that you are lying on I shall give to you and to your children.

"And your children's children shall be as many as the dust of the earth. They shall spread abroad to the west and to the east, to the north and to the south.

"And in your children shall all the families of the earth be blessed.

"I will be with you in all places where you shall go. I will take care of you and bring you back again to this land in safety. I will not leave you until I have done what I have promised."

After this surprising dream, Jacob awoke. He was astonished and somewhat afraid.

When he was able to speak, he exclaimed, "How dreadful is this place! This is the very house of God, and this is the gate of Heaven!"

Very early in the morning, Jacob took the stone that he had used for a pillow and set it up as a pillar. In this way he would be able to find the spot again when he came back. He wanted to remember the exact place where he had seen angels going up and down out of Heaven, and where God had spoken to him directly from Heaven. After he had set up the stone, he poured some oil upon it, and named the place Bethel. In his language this means *House of God.*

From that night, Jacob was a different man. He tried hard to serve God and please Him.

Jacob made a vow, a solemn promise to God. This was the vow: "If God will be with me and will keep me in the way that I go, and will give me food to eat, and clothing to put on, so that I come back safely to my father's house, then Jehovah shall be my God. This stone which I have set up for a pillar shall be God's house, and of all that the Lord shall give me, I will surely give back the tenth unto God."

Do you think that Jacob was lonely and unhappy now?

No, indeed, he was most happy. As he went on his way, he was thinking of that wonderful dream.

He was going to look for that country that the Lord had said should some day belong to him, and to his children.

He was thinking of what the Lord had said: that his descendants should be as many as the dust of the earth.

He was remembering that the Lord had said that He would never leave him; that He would go with him all the way, and would bring him back safely.

He was seeing the beautiful angels as they went up and down the ladder.

Jacob had found a friend in God, and no one is unhappy who has God for his friend.

CHAPTER 21

Jacob Meets Rachel

GENESIS 29, 30

Jacob continued his journey, a very happy man. At last he came to a place where there was a well in a field. Three flocks of sheep were lying by it, for out of that well they watered the animals. A great stone was upon the opening of the well.

There were some shepherds with the sheep. Jacob asked them, 'From what place do you come?"

"We come from Haran," they said.

Now that was the place where Jacob's uncle Laban lived. So Jacob asked them another question, "Do you know Laban?"

"Yes," they answered, "we know him."

Then Jacob asked, "Is he well?"

"Yes," they said, "he is well. Here comes his daughter Rachel now, with her sheep."

When Jacob saw Rachel, the daughter of Laban, coming near to give water to the sheep, he rolled the stone from the well's mouth, and he watered the flock for her.

Then Jacob told Rachel that he was her cousin Jacob, Rebekah's son, and he kissed her.

Rachel ran home and told her father that his sister's son had come. When Laban heard that, he too ran out to meet Jacob. He kissed Jacob and brought him to his home.

They were all very glad to see him, and Jacob stayed with them for about a month. Jacob helped Laban in whatever had to be done.

Laban said to Jacob, "If you will stay with me and help me, I will give you wages. I do not want you to work for me and earn nothing. What shall I pay you?"

Laban had two daughters. The name of the older one was Leah, and the name of the younger was Rachel. Leah was not very pretty, but Rachel was beautiful.

Jacob already loved his beautiful cousin Rachel. He said, "If you will give me Rachel, your younger daughter, to be my wife, I will serve you for seven years."

Laban said, "Very well. I would rather give her to you than to a stranger. You may stay and work for me."

Jacob served Laban seven years for Rachel, and they seemed to him only a few days, because he loved her so much. At the end of the seven years, Laban gave a big wedding and invited all the men of the place.

In that time ladies wore long veils that completely covered them, face and all, except for one eye. Laban deceived Jacob. Instead of giving Rachel to him, Laban brought his older daughter Leah. She was so covered up with her veil that Jacob did not know that it was not Rachel. But when she took off her veil, he found he had married Leah.

He went to Laban and said, "Why did you treat me in this way? Did I not serve you for Rachel? Then why have you given me Leah instead?"

Laban said: "In this country, it is not the custom to let the younger daughter get married first. If you want Rachel, however, you may have her also a week from now; but then you must work seven more years for her."

So Jacob had to work seven years longer for Rachel, whom he loved.

God did not intend that a man should have more than one wife. Having two wives caused Jacob a great deal of trouble, and led to much unhappiness. For Jacob loved Rachel much more than he loved Leah. This made Leah very sad.

When God saw that Jacob did not love Leah as much as Rachel, He gave Leah some children to comfort her.

She received four little boys, one right after the other. That made her very happy, for at that time people wanted to have children more than they wanted anything else in the world. She named them Reuben, Simeon, Levi, and Judah.

She thought that her husband Jacob would surely love her now that she was the mother of his four fine little boys.

God did not give Rachel any children. It made Rachel very unhappy to see her sister have four little boys, while she did not have any.

At last Rachel did just what Sarah, Abraham's wife, had done. She gave her maid-servant to Jacob for a wife. She thought, "Perhaps my maid, Bilhah, will have some babies, and then I can call them mine."

Jacob married Rachel's maid, Bilhah, and Bilhah received two little boys. Rachel called them hers, and she named them Dan and Naphtali.

When Leah saw what Rachel had done, she told Jacob to marry her servant, Zilpah, too. She thought, "Perhaps in that way I can get still more children."

Jacob married Zilpah, and Zilpah received two little boys. Leah called them hers, and she named them Gad and Asher.

After this, Leah had two little boys of her own. She named them Issachar and Zebulun. She was very happy now, because she had six little sons of her own, and two of her hand-maid's.

After a while, Leah received a little girl, whom she named Dinah.

Last of all, God sent Rachel a little baby boy. She was happier than she had ever been before. She named the baby Joseph.

Jacob loved Joseph best of all, because he was the son of Rachel, whom he loved, and because he was the son of his old age.

CHAPTER 22

Jacob Leaves Padan-Aram Secretly

GENESIS 31

After Joseph was born, Jacob began to think that it was about time for him to go back to his own country. He had been away twenty years — a long, long time. He did not know whether his mother and father were still alive.   He had not heard from them during all those twenty years.   Rebekah had promised to send for him when she thought that it was safe for him to come back, but she had not. Jacob did not know that she had died.

Jacob had served his uncle Laban fourteen years for his two wives, Leah and Rachel. Then he had served six years for wages.

Laban paid him in sheep and goats. He told Jacob he might have all the brown sheep and goats, and all the speckled and spotted ones. Now, it so happened when all the new little goats and lambs were born, that a great many of them were brown and speckled and spotted. Jacob of course took those for his.

So Jacob got a great many sheep and goats, and many camels and asses. He also had men-servants and maid-servants.   He was a rich man.

Indeed, he was much richer than Laban. Laban began to be jealous of Jacob. He was not pleasant to him any more, as he had been before.

About this time, the Lord spoke to Jacob in a dream and said to him, "Go back to your own land, and I will be with you."

Before he made plans to go away, Jacob wanted to see what his wives, Leah and Rachel, thought about it.   Since Laban was not friendly, he did not want him to hear what he said to them. He told them to come far out in the field, where he was taking care of the sheep.

Then he said, "I see that your father is not friendly to me any more. You know that I have worked with all my might for him, doing my very best.

"You know that he has not treated me fairly. He has cheated me ten times. But God has taken care of me, and has not let him hurt me.

"God has spoken to me in a dream, and He has said to me, 'I am the God of Bethel, where you set up a stone and poured oil upon it, and where you made a vow to Me. Now I tell you to go back to your old home, where your family lives.'"

Jacob's wives were quite content to go with him back to his old home. They answered, "Our father does not treat us well any longer either. Do whatever God has told you to do."

Jacob knew that if Laban found out that he was going away, he would not like it, and perhaps would not let him go. The only way that he could leave was to go without letting Laban know.

It happened that Laban was going away for a few days to shear his sheep.

Jacob thought that this was the time for him to leave. He got everything ready. His servants brought the camels, and Jacob put his wives and children on the backs of the animals. Joseph was only a baby. He had to be carried in his mother's arms, or perhaps in his nurse's arms when his mother was tired.

Jacob took all his household goods and all his flocks and herds, to go back to the home of his father Isaac in Canaan.

They took tents to sleep in at night, for it was a long journey of three hundred miles that they had before them. It would take them at least a month to make this long journey, with all the young animals that they had with them — the little lambs and goats, the baby asses, and baby camels.

They started off secretly, when Laban had gone to shear his sheep.

They had been gone for three days before some one told Laban that Jacob and his family had gone for good.

Laban and his brothers started after Jacob. They traveled for seven days before they caught up with him. I do not know what Laban was going to do to Jacob. But just then God appeared to Laban and told him to be very careful not to say anything threatening to Jacob.

The next day, when Laban met Jacob, he spoke very politely to him. They set up a pillar and a heap of stones. Each made a promise that he would not go past that pillar to do harm to the other. Then Laban stayed all night with Jacob. In the morning Laban kissed his two daughters and his little grandsons, and went back home to his own country, while Jacob went on.

CHAPTER 23

Jacob Goes Home

GENESIS 31, 32, 33

PART 1 — HE WRESTLES WITH GOD

Jacob was still afraid of his brother Esau. He was afraid that Esau might kill him and his family.

He sent some servants to his brother Esau to find out if Esau were angry with him still. He commanded them to speak very politely and humbly to Esau.

The messengers came back and told Jacob, "We saw your brother, and he is coming to meet you with four hundred men!"

Then Jacob became very much afraid that Esau was coming to kill him and his wives and his little children.

All those that were with them, together with the camels, the flocks, and the herds, Jacob divided into two groups, so that if Esau should come to one company and kill them all, then the other company could escape.

Then Jacob did what all people should do when they are in trouble. He prayed to God, saying, "O God of my father Abraham, and God of my father Isaac, Thou hast said to me, 'Return unto thy country and I will be with thee.' I am not worthy of all the mercies, and of all the truth which Thou hast showed to me. I was all alone when I passed over this Jordan river before, and Thou hast so blessed me that I have become two bands.

"Save me, I pray Thee, from my brother Esau, for I fear him, lest he will come and smite me, and the mother with the children."

The next day, Jacob gathered together a very fine present for Esau to see if he could not please his brother and make him friendly to him.   This was the present: two hundred she-goats and twenty he-goats; two hundred mother sheep and twenty rams; thirty mother camels, all of whom had baby camels with them; forty cows and ten bulls; and twenty asses and ten baby asses.

Was not that a pretty fine present to give Esau?   Count up all those animals, and you will see that there were five hundred eighty animals — enough to stock a large farm.   You will see that Jacob must have had a great many of his own in order to be able to give away so many.

He gave the animals to his servants — one servant for each drove, and each drove by itself.   These servants went ahead of him to meet Esau.

Jacob commanded the first servant, "When you meet my brother Esau, and he asks, 'Who are you? Where are you going? Whose animals are these?' then I want you to say very politely, 'These belong to your servant Jacob. He has sent them for a present to my lord Esau. He himself is coming behind us.' "

Jacob told the second servant, who was driving the second flock, to say the same thing. The other servants were to repeat what the first two had said.

The droves of animals started. The second driver waited till the first one was perhaps a mile ahead, and then he started.

This was to surprise Esau. He would think that the first one was the only present. Of course, when he saw the second one coming over the hill, he would be surprised; and then when the others came, he would be still more surprised.

There was a little river, called the Jabbok, in the place where they lodged that night. After all the droves had passed over the Jabbok, Jacob sent his two wives and the two maid-servants and his children after them.

But Jacob himself did not go over the brook. He stayed behind.

Jacob must have been more afraid than he had ever been in all his life. He wanted to be all alone so that he could pray to God to help him.

While Jacob stayed behind, a man came and wrestled with Jacob the whole night long. Jacob wrestled so hard that he almost overcame the man. When the visitor saw how hard Jacob wrestled, he showed that he was not a man at all, but a heavenly visitor. He touched the hollow of Jacob's thigh, and the touch made Jacob's thigh out of joint, so that he became lame. Of course, then he could not wrestle very well.

The heavenly visitor said, "Let me go, for the day is breaking."

Jacob, now knowing that his visitor came from Heaven and could help in his troubles, said, "I will not let Thee go unless Thou bless me first."

How different Jacob was from Esau, who had let his birthright go for a little dish of soup! Jacob fought hard to get a blessing.

The heavenly visitor said to him, "What is your name?"

Jacob said, 'My name is Jacob."

The visitor said, "Your name shall no more be Jacob. Your name shall be Israel, because you have wrestled with God and men. This name means *a Prince of God.*" Then the visitor blessed Jacob.

Jacob knew now that his heavenly visitor was God Himself, who had come to bless him. Jacob called the name of that place Peniel, which means *the Face of God.* "For," said Jacob, "I have seen God face to face."

Part 2 — He Meets Esau

When the sun rose, Jacob passed over the brook to join his family, who had gone before him. He could not walk without limping on the foot where the Lord had touched the sinew of the thigh. He stayed lame all the rest of his life. But his lameness only made him remember that wonderful night when he had seen the Lord face to face.

After Jacob and his family had gone some distance, they saw a cloud of dust far off. Soon they saw that it was Esau and his company of men.

They were badly frightened, you may be sure.

Jacob put the two hand-maids and their children ahead; and Leah and her children next; and Rachel and Joseph last of all, so that if Esau meant to do them any harm, he would do it first to the two hand-maids and their children, and perhaps to Leah and her children. In this way, Rachel and Joseph might have a chance to escape.

Then Jacob himself went first. He bowed himself right down to the ground, not once, but seven times, till he came near to his brother Esau.

Esau did not bow down to Jacob. He got down from his camel — and what do you think he did? He ran to meet Jacob, and he hugged and kissed him. They both cried with joy to see each other. Both of them forgot that they had ever been angry with each other. They remembered only that they were twin brothers.

After a little while Esau saw the women and children. He asked, "Whose are these?"

Jacob said, "The children which God hath graciously given me."

Then the two hand-maids came near with their children, and bowed themselves low to Esau. Next Leah came near and bowed; and last of all Rachel and little Joseph came, and they too bowed low.

Esau asked, "What are all these droves of animals that I have met?"

Jacob said, "They are a present for my lord."

Esau answered, "I have enough, my brother. Keep these for yourself."

When Jacob insisted, Esau took the present.

Esau suggested that now he and Jacob should travel together. But Jacob did not quite like that plan. He was still a little bit afraid of Esau; he said that Esau had better go ahead, for Jacob's family had to travel very slowly because of the small children and cattle with them.

So they parted. Esau went on to the place where he lived, Mount Seir. Jacob went into the land of Canaan, toward Hebron, where his father Isaac was still living, now a very old man.

As Jacob journeyed, he came to the same place where he had lain down to sleep when he was running away from his brother, twenty years before.

You remember that Jacob set up the stone which he had used for a pillow, and that he named the place Bethel, or *House of God*.

Now Jacob stopped at Bethel. He built an altar and worshipped God there.

Again he continued his journey to Hebron. He longed to see his old father, all the more since his mother Rebekah had died.

But before Jacob reached Hebron, something very sad happened. His wife Rachel, whom he loved dearly, became ill and died.

Just before she died, God sent her another baby boy. His father called him Benjamin. It is no wonder that his father loved little Benjamin very much. Joseph and Benjamin were Rachel's children, and Jacob loved them because he had loved her.

They buried Rachel there, and Jacob set up a pillar to mark the grave.

After Rachel's funeral they came at last to Hebron, where Isaac still lived.

Isaac was over one hundred years old when Jacob went away, and Jacob had been gone for twenty years. His father was now about one hundred sixty years old. He lived twenty years longer, and was able to talk to his grand-children, Jacob's twelve sons. He taught them about God, telling them all about the wonderful promises that He had made to their great-grandfather Abraham.

At last Isaac's life ended. He was one hundred eighty years old when he died. His sons, Jacob and Esau, buried him in the Cave of Machpelah, where Abraham and Sarah and Rebekah were buried.

A little town grew up near the pillar that marked Rachel's grave. The town was called Bethlehem. Who was born in Bethlehem hundreds of years later?

CHAPTER 24

How Joseph Was Sold

GENESIS 37

Jacob lived in the land of Canaan, where his father had lived. When Joseph was a young boy seventeen years old, the other brothers were grown-up men.

They were shepherds, pasturing their father's flocks. Often they had to travel about to find enough grass for the flocks. Sometimes Joseph went with them.

Jacob loved Joseph more than all his other children, because he was the son of Rachel. He gave Joseph a coat of many beautiful colors. Probably it was of silk cloth, skillfully embroidered.

When the other brothers saw that their father loved Joseph more than them, they were jealous. They hated Joseph and could not speak kindly to him.

Once Joseph dreamed a strange dream which he told to his brothers. He dreamed that they were in the field, binding the grain into bundles, and his sheaf stood up, while all the rest of the sheaves came and bowed down to his.

His brothers were very angry when they heard him say this. They said, "Indeed, and do you think that this dream means that you are going to rule over us?" They hated him still more because of the dream.

Joseph dreamed another time. Again he told the dream to his brothers and his father. "This time," he said, "I dreamed that I saw the sun, and the moon, and eleven stars, and they all came and bowed down to me."

In those days, dreams often told what would happen in the future. The brothers became still more jealous, but Jacob began to wonder what his son's strange dreams might mean.

Joseph's wonderful dreams really did mean something. They came true, many years later. First many strange things happened to him.

Soon after the dreams, Joseph's brothers went to pasture their flocks in Shechem, a place quite far from Jacob's home.

After they had been there for some time, their father Jacob wanted to know how they were getting along. He told Joseph to go and see if they were well, and then to come back and tell his father all that he had found out.

When Joseph came to Shechem, he looked around for his brothers. There was no sign of them.

At last a man found him wandering in the field, and asked him, "What are you looking for?"

"I am looking for my brothers," said Joseph. "Can you tell me where to find them?"

"They were here," said the man, "but they have gone away, for I heard them say, 'Let us go to Dothan.'"

So Joseph went to Dothan. At last he found his brothers there. They saw him coming across the fields, while he was still far away, and they made a wicked plan.

They said to each other, "Here comes this dreamer. Let us kill him, and cast his body into some dark hole. Then we shall see what will become of his dreams! We will tell our father that a wild beast has eaten him."

Reuben, the oldest brother, was not so wicked and cruel as the others.

He said, "Let us not kill him. Let us cast him into this dark hole, instead of shedding his blood."

Reuben planned to take Joseph out of the pit, when the others were not around, and take him back to his father.

When Joseph came near, they pounced upon the poor boy and took off his beautiful coat of many colors. Then they let him down into an empty pit, from which he could not get out.

Poor Joseph was badly frightened in this dark hole. He cried out, begging them to take him up. But the wicked brothers left him down in the hole.

They sat down to eat their dinner, just as if their brother were not crying and calling to them.

While they were eating their meal, they saw a cloud of dust in the distance. Pretty soon they could see that it was a group of camels and people. The people were Ishmaelites on their way to Egypt. Their camels were loaded with spices, balm, and myrrh, which they were going to sell in Egypt.

Judah, one of the brothers, said to the others, "What good will it do us to kill our brother? Let us sell him to these Ishmaelites. After all, he is our brother."

The rest thought that this would be a good way to get rid of Joseph. They were sure that if they sold him to these men, who were going far away, he would never bother them again.

By the time they had agreed to sell him, the Ishmaelites were near. The brothers called to them to stop, because they had a young boy whom they wanted to sell as a slave.

Pharaoh had his servants dress Joseph in beautiful clothes. Genesis 41

Joseph was a hundred and ten years old when he died. Genesis 50

Every week his mother took him to Pharaoh's palace. Exodus 2

The taskmasters beat them. Exodus 5

That did not seem strange to the Ishmaelites, for it was the custom to buy and sell slaves.

Twenty pieces of silver was the price the Ishmaelites paid for Joseph. His brothers went to the dark hole and drew the boy up.

Joseph thought, at first, that they were going to let him go free. How bitterly disappointed he must have been when he found that he was to be sold as a slave!

In vain he begged them to let him go home to his father. He was to be taken down to far-away Egypt, where he would probably never see his dear father again. His brothers put him on one of the camels, and the Ishmaelites went on their journey, carrying him farther and farther away from his home.

Reuben, the oldest brother, was not with the others when Joseph was sold. He came back, intending to take Joseph out of the hole secretly and send him back to his father. When he could not find Joseph, he thought that his brothers had killed him.

He tore his clothes, as people did in those days when they felt very sad, and he cried out, "The child is dead, and I, what shall I do?" He knew that his father would hold him responsible, because he was the oldest.

The brothers killed a goat and dipped Joseph's coat in the blood. When they reached home, they took the bloody coat to their father. They lied, "We found this coat. Look and see whether it is your son's."

Jacob knew that it was Joseph's coat. He cried out very sorrowfully, "It is my son's coat. Some wild animal must have eaten him. Joseph is without doubt torn in pieces."

Jacob tore his clothes, and put sack-cloth on his body. He mourned for Joseph so long that his sons and daughters began to fear that he would never get over it. They tried to comfort him, but it was of no use. He said, "I will go down into the grave to my son, mourning."

The wicked brothers added to their sin by not telling the truth to their poor old father. They let him believe that Joseph had really been torn to pieces by some wild beast. This was just as bad as telling a lie.

Although their father could not know how wicked his sons were, God knew all about it. He punished them in later years for their sins.

CHAPTER 25

In Potiphar's House

GENESIS 39, 40

Joseph traveled with the Ishmaelites for many long days. Finally, after a long journey through the hot desert, they came to the fertile land of Egypt. There everything was beautiful and green, watered by the mighty Nile river.

Here Joseph was sold as a slave to a rich soldier named Potiphar, who was the captain of Pharaoh's guard. Pharaoh was the king of the land of Egypt. Of course, since Potiphar was one of his high officers, he lived in a very fine house, and had a great many servants.

This was a strange life to Joseph. Before, he had been the favorite son, helping care for his father's sheep. Now he was only a slave in the beautiful home of a rich man.

His life was changed in a more important way. Now he was in a heathen country, where God was not known. The Egyptian people worshipped the sun.

Joseph was only seventeen years old when he was taken down to Egypt. He was surrounded by heathen people, who knew nothing about God. All worshipped idols. Did he soon learn to worship idols? Did he forget the God of his fathers, Abraham, Isaac, and Jacob?

No, he never forgot God. He remembered what his father and mother and grandfather Isaac had taught him about God. He still prayed. Joseph must have learned his lessons about God well, when his father and mother taught him. He must have learned to pray while he was a young boy.

He never had another chance to learn about God.

Joseph was not alone, although he was far from home. God stayed with Joseph. Everything that he did prospered. When Potiphar saw that everything that Joseph did went well, he let Joseph manage the whole household.

Now, Joseph was a handsome young man. His mother, Rachel, had been very beautiful, and Joseph looked much like her. Because he was good-looking, Potiphar's wife fell in love with him. Of course, this was wrong, because she was a married woman. Joseph knew it was wrong, and he would not listen to her.

Potiphar's wicked wife, when she found that she could not make Joseph sin, began to hate him. She told her husband lying stories about him.

Potiphar believed his wife. It was of no use for Joseph to say the stories were not true, for he was only a slave. Naturally, Potiphar believed his wife.

Joseph was put into the prison where the king's prisoners were kept. His feet were bound with iron fetters which hurt very much.

It was hard for Joseph to be in prison for doing good instead of evil; but after all, it was going to turn out well. God was taking care of Joseph all the time, and God had a wonderful plan for Joseph's life, as you will see.

Although Joseph was in prison, he did not have a hard time, because God soon made the keeper of the prison friendly to him. This man put him in charge of all the other prisoners, and trusted everything in the prison to him. The Lord was with Joseph here, too, making everything that he did to prosper.

While Joseph was in prison, two of the king's servants were sent there. They had done something to make the king angry.

One of them was the king's chief butler, who waited on the table; and the other was the king's chief baker, who prepared the food for the king to eat. These two men were put under Joseph's care.

One night each of them dreamed a strange dream. When Joseph came to see them in the morning, he found them looking worried and sad, for there was no one to tell them what the dreams might mean.

In Egypt, too, people thought that a dream was sent to foretell something that was going to happen.

Joseph said to them, "God can tell what these dreams mean. Tell me the dreams, I pray you."

The chief butler told his dream to Joseph. He said, "In my dream I saw a grape vine which had three branches, with blossoms and ripe grapes on it. And Pharaoh's cup was in my hand, and I took the grapes and squeezed them into Pharaoh's cup, and gave the cup to Pharaoh to drink from."

Joseph said, "This is what your dream means. The three branches are three days. In three days Pharaoh will take you out of the prison, and will make you his butler again. You shall give Pharaoh his cup again, as you used to.

"Don't forget me when you come into favor. Remember me, and tell Pharaoh about me, so he will get me out of prison. Truly, I was stolen out of the land of the Hebrews. Since I have been in Egypt, I have done nothing that I should be put into this prison."

When the chief baker saw that the interpretation of the butler's dream was good, he told Joseph his dream. "I dreamed that I had three white baskets on my head, and the top basket was filled with all kinds of good baked foods for Pharaoh to eat. The birds came and ate up all the food out of the basket."

Then Joseph said, "This is what your dream means. The three baskets are three days. In three days Pharaoh shall lift your head off, and shall hang you upon a tree, and the birds shall eat your flesh."

It happened that Pharaoh had a birthday three days later. He gave a feast to all his servants. He sent for the chief butler and the chief baker.

He restored the chief butler to his position. As Joseph had said, the butler waited upon Pharaoh's table again, and gave Pharaoh his cup.

And Pharaoh hanged the chief baker, as Joseph had foretold.

But the chief butler did not remember Joseph. He forgot all about him.

CHAPTER 26

From Prison to Palace

GENESIS 41

PART 1 — PHARAOH'S DREAM

Poor Joseph was left in the dungeon. How unkind of the butler to forget all about him!

He was there two years, and then God made something happen which brought a great change in Joseph's life.

This is what happened. The great king of Egypt himself had a dream. It was a very strange one. It was a double dream.

Pharaoh dreamed that he stood by the river. He saw seven very fine fat cows coming up out of the river. They went into a meadow and began to graze. Afterward, he saw seven thin, starved-looking cows coming up out of the river. The seven thin, starved-looking cows ate up the seven fat ones.

After he had dreamed this, Pharaoh woke up. He went to sleep and dreamed again.

This time he thought he saw seven fine fat ears of grain come up on one stalk. After them came up seven thin ears, blasted with the east wind. And the seven thin ears ate up the seven full ears.

Pharaoh woke up again, and found that it was a dream.

In the morning, Pharaoh was very much troubled about his dream. He called for all the magicians and wise men of Egypt to tell him the meaning of his dream.

The magicians and wise men were supposed to be able to tell the meaning of dreams. So Pharaoh told them what he had seen.

The wise men thought and thought. At last they shook their heads and said, "O great and mighty king, we cannot interpret the dream."

Now there was great trouble in the court. No one could interpret the king's dream.

Then all at once the chief butler remembered Joseph, who had told him the meaning of his dream in prison. He spoke to Pharaoh and said, "I remember the day that Pharaoh was angry with the chief baker and me. He put us both into prison. While we were there, we each dreamed one night. In the prison there was a young Hebrew. We told him our dreams, and he told us the meaning of our dreams. What he said came true. I was taken back to be the king's butler, and the baker was hanged."

When Pharaoh heard this, he sent for Joseph. The messengers ran to the prison quickly. They told Joseph that the king wanted him. So Joseph shaved himself and put on his best clothes. Then he went to the palace. Pharaoh said to him, "I have dreamed a dream, and there is no one in all my kingdom who can interpret it. I have been told that you can understand dreams and interpret them."

Joseph answered humbly, "It is not in me. I have no power to understand them. But in God is all power. God will give Pharaoh an answer of peace."

Then Pharaoh told his dream to Joseph, about the seven thin cows that ate up the seven fat ones, and the seven poor ears of grain that ate up the seven fine ones.

Joseph answered the great king carefully, choosing his words, because it is not polite to say *you* to a king. When he meant *you*, he had to say *Pharaoh*.

He said, "The two dreams which Pharaoh has had are just one dream, for they mean one thing. It is God who has sent these dreams. God has given Pharaoh the honor of revealing to him what He is soon going to do.

"The seven good cows and the seven fine ears of grain shall be seven years. They have the same meaning. And the seven thin and ill-favored cows and the seven empty, blasted ears of grain shall be another seven years.

"Behold, there are coming seven years of wonderful harvests throughout the whole land of Egypt. In these seven plentiful years, the earth will bring forth much food, so that the people will not know what to do with it.

"And after the seven plentiful years are over, there will come seven years of terrible famine, when nothing will grow at all! The seven years of famine will be so severe that the people will forget that there ever were any years of rich harvests.

"The reason that Pharaoh dreamed the dream twice is that God will surely bring all this to pass, and that very soon."

After Joseph had told Pharaoh the meaning of his dreams, he told Pharaoh what to do for the future.

He said, "Now let Pharaoh try to find a man who is very wise, and let Pharaoh make him ruler of the whole country. Let Pharaoh appoint officers to rule the country. When those seven plentiful years come, let the officers gather up one-fifth of the food of those good years, and store it up in barns, so as to keep it safe till the seven years of famine come. Then when the bad years come, there will be enough food to keep the people from starving."

PART 2 — JOSEPH'S REWARD

Pharaoh was very much pleased with Joseph's advice. He said to his servants, "We cannot find another man so wise as this Joseph is, for the Spirit of God is in him."

Then Pharaoh said to Joseph, "Because God has showed you all this, there is no one who is so wise and sensible as you are. So I will appoint you to be the ruler over the land of Egypt, as you have said. Whatever you say must be obeyed. I shall still be the king, but you will do all the ruling."

Pharaoh took off his royal ring from his hand, and put it upon Joseph's hand.

If Joseph should want to make a law, he must put some soft wax on the paper, and then press the seal of the ring down upon the soft wax. There would be the mark of the king's seal in the wax. Everyone would know that the command on the paper must be obeyed, for it had the king's seal upon it.

If Joseph were going to be a high ruler, he must be very handsomely dressed. Pharaoh had his servants dress Joseph in splendid clothes. He put a heavy gold chain around Joseph's neck.

He also gave Joseph a chariot to ride in when he was driving around the country. A chariot was a horse-drawn car. There was only one in the whole kingdom that was handsomer than Joseph's — and that was Pharaoh's own.

Pharaoh appointed some servants to run before Joseph's chariot, and to cry to all the people, "Bow the knee!" All the people in the street must fall down on their knees till Joseph's chariot passed by, just as they did when Pharaoh's chariot passed.

Of course, now that Joseph had become a great man, he must have a fine name, too. The king named him Zaphnath-Paaneah, which means in the Egyptian language, *The man to whom secrets are revealed.*

Joseph must also have a wife. So Pharaoh gave him a princess named Asenath for his wife. She was the daughter of the priest of the city of On, which is now called Memphis.

Joseph lived in a magnificent palace. He had a great many servants, was dressed in rich clothing, and rode in the second best chariot in the kingdom. Wherever he went, he was treated with great respect.

Soon God gave him another blessing. God gave him two little sons. He named the first one Manasseh, which means *Forgetting.* He said "God has given me so many good things, that He has made me forget all the trouble that I had before."

The second one he named Ephraim, which means *Fruitful.* He said, "God has made me fruitful in this land."

Joseph was now thirty years old. Instead of being a Hebrew slave boy, he was now an Egyptian prince. It was God who planned Joseph's life, and made all these wonderful things happen to him.

Meanwhile the seven plenteous years came. The earth brought forth bountiful harvests, far more than the people could use. No one had ever seen such rich harvests before.

Joseph built big barns in which he stored the grain which he gathered. There was so much food that it could not be counted. Around every city there were enormous granaries, filled to the roof with grain.

At last the seven years of plenty were ended, and the seven years of famine began to come. The famine was not only in Egypt, but in every land. When the people planted their seed, nothing came up. In other lands, the people had not known about the seven years of famine, and so they had not saved up anything during the seven years of plenty. Now they were beginning to suffer from hunger.

But in the land of Egypt there was bread.

When the fields would not grow any grain, the people cried to Pharaoh for bread. He answered all of them, "Go to Joseph, and do whatever he tells you."

When the famine became so severe that the people were beginning to suffer for want of food, Joseph opened all the store houses and sold grain to the Egyptians.

When the people in all the other countries heard that there was grain in Egypt, they came there to buy it. Everybody wanted the food which Joseph had stored during the years of plenty.

CHAPTER 27

Joseph's Dreams Come True

GENESIS 42

PART 1 — HE MEETS HIS BROTHERS

Joseph was a young lad about seventeen years old when he was carried down to Egypt by the Ishmaelites and sold as a slave to Potiphar. Now he was thirty years old.

Meanwhile, what had been happening to his father and brothers? His father was becoming an old man. All of his brothers, except little Benjamin, were married, with wives and children of their own.

The famine was in the land of Canaan, as well as in other countries. Jacob and his family were in great distress because they had not enough food. They did not know what to do. Joseph's brothers looked at each other and said, "What shall we do to get food? The little that we have will soon be gone, and then we and our little ones will starve."

But Jacob, their father, had heard that there was grain down in Egypt. So he said to his sons, "Why are you looking so anxiously at each other? I have heard that in Egypt there is food. Go down there and buy us some, so that we will not starve."

Jacob's ten oldest sons went down to Egypt to buy food. Benjamin did not go with them, for his father was afraid to let him go on a long journey. He might meet with harm, as Joseph had. So his father kept him at home.

One day, as Joseph was selling grain to all the men who came to buy, he looked up and saw ten men from his own country, the land of Canaan. They came, like all the others, and bowed themselves before him with their faces to the earth. It was the custom for men in that country to bow thus before a great lord.

Suddenly Joseph saw that the ten men from the land of Canaan were his own brothers!

He knew them, for they looked just the same as when he had seen them last, except that they were a little older. They wore just the same kind of clothes. They also spoke Hebrew, and Joseph understood all that they said.

But they did not know him. How could they? He had been only a young boy when they had seen him last. They had sold him to be a slave, and no doubt they thought he was still a slave, working for some master in Egypt. They did not expect to see him in Egypt. And certainly they did not expect to see him as a ruler in the kingdom of Egypt, the highest ruler except Pharaoh himself!

When they had sold him to be a slave, he was dressed as a simple Hebrew shepherd boy. Now he was gorgeously dressed as an Egyptian prince, with a heavy gold chain around his neck, and the king's signet ring on his finger.

Joseph did not tell them who he was. He wanted to find out if they were still as cruel as they had been when they sold him.

So he did not speak to them in Hebrew, but in Egyptian. An interpreter, who understood both Egyptian and Hebrew, told the brothers what the great lord said, by saying it in Hebrew.

Joseph thought it would do them good to be afraid of him, and to realize, when they found out who he was, that he was powerful enough to have them punished for their cruelty to him as a boy.

He spoke roughly to them, so as to frighten them: "Where do you men come from?"

After the interpreter had told them what Joseph said, they answered, "We come from the land of Canaan to buy food."

Joseph suddenly remembered his dreams, about the eleven sheaves of wheat which bowed down to his sheaf, and about the sun and the moon and the eleven stars which bowed down to him. Joseph saw that his dreams had come true at last.

He kept on talking roughly to his brothers. "No, no, you did not come down here to buy food. You came to spy out the land. You must be spies, and you came here to find out how your country can make war on us."

The brothers were very much frightened. If this great lord thought they were spies, he would have them all hanged, for spies were always hanged when they were caught! They answered very humbly, "No, no, my lord. We are not spies. We have come to buy food."

But Joseph would not listen to them, "I tell you that you are spies. You have come to spy out the country, and to make trouble."

The brothers were terrified. "My lord, we are your servants. We are all good men. We are brothers, and we are the sons of one man. The youngest is still at home with our father, and one is dead."

Joseph would not believe them. He said, "I tell you that you are spies, but I will give you a chance to prove that what you say is true. If you have a younger brother as you say, you must send one of you back to get him. You must bring him here, so that I can see if what you say is true. For by the life of Pharaoh, you shall not be allowed to leave the land of Egypt, unless your younger brother come here first.

"Send one of you back to your home to bring your brother here. I will keep you in prison till he comes back with your youngest brother, so that I can prove whether there is any truth in what you say. If you have not spoken the truth, then you are spies."

Joseph put all his brothers into prison for three days. It was good for them to have a little punishment. It made them remember how cruel they had been to Joseph.

PART 2 — THE BROTHERS RETURN HOME

After three days, Joseph let them out of prison. He said to them, "I will not keep you all in prison, for I believe in God. I will keep only one of you here. The rest may go back and carry food to your families, for they may be starving. When you need more food, you must bring your youngest brother with you. Then I will know that you are speaking the truth."

Joseph's word worried the brothers. They knew that their father would not let Benjamin go, and they did not see how they could ever come back for more food.

They said to each other, "It is our punishment for treating our brother Joseph so cruelly. We would not let him go, when he begged us. Now God is punishing us."

Then Reuben spoke. It had been Reuben, you remember, who tried to save Joseph from the others, and who told them to put him into the pit, intending to come and rescue him when the others were gone. Now he said, "Did I not tell you not to sin against the boy? You would not listen. Now we have to suffer for what we did."

They did not know that Joseph could understand what they were saying, because he always spoke in the Egyptian language when he talked with them.

When Joseph heard them talking together, and saying that this was a just punishment for the way they had treated him, his heart softened. He remembered that, after all, they were his brothers, whom he had not seen for fifteen years. He felt that he loved them still. He could not keep from weeping from homesickness. He had to go into another room, because he could not keep the tears from rolling down his cheeks.

Yet he did not want to tell them who he was. They were not sorry enough. He knew that they would soon come back again to buy grain. Then he would tell them who he was.

How he longed to see Benjamin! Benjamin was his own brother, whereas all the others were only half-brothers. That is why he insisted that they must bring Benjamin when they should come again.

Joseph wiped his tears away and went back to his brothers. He talked with them. Then he took Simeon, and bound him before their eyes, and put him in prison.

Joseph commanded his servants to fill their sacks with grain. He did not want to take pay from his brothers; so he told his servants to put the money back again into their sacks.

Now the brothers were free to go home again, though they must go without Simeon. After loading the sacks of grain on their donkeys, they started on the homeward journey.

On the way, one of them opened his sack to give his donkey some food. To his great surprise, he found his money at the opening of the sack!

He called to the others, "My money has been given back! Here it is in my sack!"

They were frightened. They said, "What has God done to us?" for they knew that nothing can happen unless God sends it.

At last they reached home, where their old father was anxiously waiting for them. Of course, they told him all that had happened to them — that the ruler had said they were spies, that he had put Simeon in prison until they should come for more food, bringing Benjamin with them.

Then they emptied their sacks. What was their surprise to find that every one's money was in his sack!

Their poor old father felt very sad when he listened to their story. He became most sorrowful when they said that they could not go back again unless their brother Benjamin went with them.

"You are making me lose my children," he said pitifully. "Joseph is dead, and Simeon is in Egypt. Now you want to rob me of Benjamin, too. All these things are against me."

Then Reuben, who was the oldest of the brothers, and who seemed to be the most responsible, said to his father, "I myself will take charge of Benjamin, and I promise surely to bring him back to you safely. If I do not, you may kill my two sons."

Reuben knew that his father would never want to kill his two little boys, but he hoped that if he made such a strong promise, his father would let Benjamin go.

But it did no good. The old father only said, "No, Benjamin shall not go with you, for his brother Joseph is dead, and if anything happens to Benjamin on the way, you will bring down my gray hairs with sorrow to the grave."

CHAPTER 28

Benjamin Goes to Egypt

GENESIS 43

The family of Jacob lived on the grain that had been bought in Egypt. They hoped that when they planted their fields the next year, the famine would be over, and that plenty of grain would come up. They did not know, as Joseph did, that the dreadful famine was going to last seven long years.

The next year they planted their fields, but almost nothing came up. It was another year of famine.

By and by they had eaten up almost all their food. Their father said to them, "Go again, and buy us a little food."

But Judah said to his father, "The man told us, 'You shall not see my face, unless you bring your youngest brother with you.' If you will let Benjamin go with us, we will go down and buy more food. If you will not let Benjamin go, we will not go."

Poor old Jacob said, "Why did you treat me so badly, telling the man that you had a young brother?"

They answered, "But the man asked us all about ourselves. He wanted to know if our father were still alive, and if we had another brother. We only answered his questions. How could we know that he would say, 'Bring your brother down'?"

Judah said, "Send him with me. I promise to take care of him. If I do not bring him back to you, I will bear the blame. If we had not waited so long, we could have gone and come back by now."

Their father saw that he would have to let Benjamin go, or they would all die of starvation. They had hardly enough food to last till the brothers could get back again.

He said, "If it must be so, take him. But give the man a present. Take a little balm, a little honey, some spices, some nuts and almonds. And take double money in your hand. Perhaps it was a mistake that your money was returned in your sacks.

"And God Almighty give you mercy before the man, that he may send back Simeon and Benjamin."

The brothers took the present, and double money, and they soon were on their way to Egypt with Benjamin.

When Joseph saw the brothers, and Benjamin with them, his heart leaped with joy. There he was — his own brother, Benjamin! He told his servant to take the men to his home, and make ready a fine feast, for they were to have dinner with him that day.

Joseph's brothers were very much alarmed when they were taken to his house. They thought they were going to be punished for having the money in their sacks.

They came trembling to the steward of Joseph's house, telling him that they had brought back the money which they found in their sacks.

But the steward, instead of treating them roughly, as they expected, spoke very kindly to them and said, "Peace be to you! Fear not. Your God, and the God of your father, gave you treasure in your sacks. I had your money."

Then he brought Simeon out of the prison to them.

After leading them into Joseph's palace, the steward told a servant to get some water so they could wash their hot and dusty feet. The steward also gave their asses something to eat.

The brothers began to feel more comfortable. They lost all their fear when they were told that Joseph had invited them to have dinner with him that noon. But they wondered what it could mean.

As soon as Joseph came home, they gave him the present. They bowed down to the earth before him, making the finest, lowest bow they knew.

When Joseph saw his own brother, Benjamin, in his house, he wanted to run to him and hug him. Instead, he asked them, "Is this your youngest brother of whom you spoke to me?"

Then he turned to Benjamin, "God be gracious to thee, my son."

Tears began to roll down his cheeks, and he hurried into his bedroom because he could not stop them. After a while he could again control his feelings. He washed his face, and went back to his brothers.

He commanded the steward, "Bring the dinner on." The steward set three tables. The first one was for Joseph alone, because the high lords always ate by themselves. The second table was for the brothers. The third one was for the Egyptians who ate with Joseph, for they would never eat at the same table with Hebrews.

The steward seated the brothers according to their age, the oldest first, and then the next, and so on to the youngest, who was seated last. This surprised the brothers, for they could not understand how he knew how old they were.

Joseph sent good things to their table as they ate. When he sent food to Benjamin, however, it was five times as much as he sent to any of the others. They enjoyed themselves very much. But still Joseph did not tell them who he was.

CHAPTER 29

Joseph's Silver Cup

GENESIS 44, 45

After the dinner was finished, Joseph commanded the steward to fill the sacks of the brothers with grain, as much as they would hold. His own silver cup was put at the top of the sack of the youngest. Every one's money was put back at the top of his sack.

The men must start for home early in the morning, because the family at home had very little food left.

As soon as it was light, the brothers started out. When they were not yet far away from the city, Joseph commanded his steward, "Hurry and go after these men. As soon as you overtake them, say to them, 'Why have you paid back evil for good? Why have you stolen my lord's silver cup? You have done wrong in taking the cup.'"

The steward hurried after the men. As soon as he overtook them, he called out, "Why have you done such a thing as to steal my lord's silver cup when you were so nicely treated? That was a very wrong thing to do."

The brothers were astonished. They answered, "Why do you speak like this to us? God forbid that we should do such a thing. Didn't we bring back the money that we found in our sacks before? If we did that, why should we now steal silver or gold out of your master's house?"

They were so sure that none of them had stolen it, that they said, "You may search our sacks. If you find that any one of us has stolen it, you may put him to death, and all of us will be my lord's slaves."

The steward said, "Very well, I shall do as you say. But I shall not take all of you for slaves. I shall take only the one who has stolen the cup."

The brothers hurried to show him that he was mistaken. Very quickly each one of them took down his sack to the ground and opened it.

The steward looked into every man's sack, beginning with the oldest, and going on till he reached the youngest. There, on the top, in Benjamin's sack, was the silver cup!

Oh, what horror came into the hearts of the brothers! How had the cup come into Benjamin's sack? It was as mysterious as the way in which their money had come back into their sacks.

What were they to do? In their distress they tore their clothes.

They could not let Benjamin go back with the steward to become an Egyptian slave. They had treated Joseph in that way, but they had learned a lesson since then. They had seen how bad their father had felt when Joseph was carried away, and they knew that their father would die if Benjamin did not come back.

They strapped the bags of grain on the backs of the asses. Then they turned around and went back with the steward to Joseph's house.

Joseph was at home. All the brothers fell down before him on the ground, bowing very humbly indeed! He looked at his eleven brothers, bowing with their heads to the ground, and he said to them, "What a way for you to behave, after you have been treated so nicely! To steal my silver cup! Do you not know that I am able to find out your secret things?"

Judah, who had promised his father that he would surely bring Benjamin back, said, "We do not know what to say to my lord. How can we excuse ourselves? We will all be my lord's slaves."

"No," said Joseph. "It would not be right for me to take you all for slaves. I will take only that one in whose sack the cup was found. The rest of you may go home again to your father."

This did not comfort the brothers. If any of them went home, it must be Benjamin. Their father would die if Benjamin did not return.

Judah stepped a little closer to Joseph. Then he made a long explanation and entreaty, saying that Benjamin was their father's youngest and best-loved son, and that if anything should happen to him, their father would die of grief. He offered to stay behind and be Joseph's servant, if he would only let Benjamin go.

Joseph had been busy supplying people with food. Perhaps he had not thought how his old father in Canaan was grieving for the loss of his son Joseph. Now, when he heard Judah tell about his father's sorrow for his lost son, and heard how he dreaded to have Benjamin go down to Egypt, his heart softened. When he heard how much his old father still loved him, he could stand it no longer.

He did not want the Egyptians to see him break down with weeping; so he commanded all the Egyptians to leave the room.

Then he told his brothers who he was. He could hardly speak for tears. He cried so loudly that all the Egyptians in the other room heard him.

"I am Joseph," he said. "Is my father still living?"

But his brothers were so much surprised that they could not answer. Was this grand man their brother Joseph whom they had sold into Egypt to be a slave? They could not believe it.

Joseph told them to come nearer to him, and not to be afraid or angry with themselves for having sold him, for it was God's plan to send him to Egypt, to save lives during the famine. There had been two years of famine, but five years were still to come.

He told his brothers to go back to their father and tell him that Joseph invited him to come to Egypt while the famine should last, and he would give them food.

After Joseph had said all this, his brothers began to believe what he said. Joseph threw his arms around his own dear brother Benjamin. He hugged and kissed him, weeping. Then Joseph kissed all his other brothers, with tears rolling down his cheeks.

Joseph's brothers were no longer afraid of him. They spent a long time talking with him.

CHAPTER 30

Israel Goes to Egypt

GENESIS 45, 46, 47

PART 1 — THE GOOD NEWS

The Egyptians in the other room wondered what all this meant. Why did they hear this noise of crying?

Soon they learned that the men were Joseph's brothers. Then there was great excitement among them. The news reached Pharaoh's palace. When Pharaoh heard it he was pleased.

Everyone thought so much of Joseph that all the people were glad that happiness had come to him. Along the street, everyone was calling out, "Have you heard that Joseph's brothers have come?"

Pharaoh said to Joseph, "Tell your brothers to go back to the land of Canaan, and to bring your father and their families to this country. I will give you the best of the land of Egypt.

"Take wagons out of the land of Egypt, to carry your little ones and your wives and your father. Do not bother to bring all your household goods, for you can have the best that there is in the land of Egypt."

How kind and gracious Pharaoh was to Joseph's brothers! He felt that Joseph had done so much for Egypt, that he was glad to be able to do something for Joseph in return.

Joseph sent wagons along with his brothers, so that his old father and all the women and children could ride to Egypt. He also gave them all they needed for the journey. And he gave each a present — each of the older brothers a suit of clothes, and Benjamin five suits of clothes and three hundred pieces of silver.

Joseph sent a present along for his old father, too — ten asses loaded with the most delicious things to eat; and ten asses loaded with grain, bread, and meat for his father and his family to use on the journey.

How eager the brothers were to get back to their father and tell him the wonderful news! All the way home they kept saying, "What will Father say when we tell him?"

Far off in the land of Canaan, poor old Israel was sitting alone in his tent door. He was thinking of his dear boy Joseph, so long lost to him, and saying to himself, as he had said so many times before, "He was surely torn to pieces by some wild beast. Benjamin, too, is gone, and perhaps I shall never see him again."

He was praying, "Oh, God, bring back my boy. Do not let me lose him, as I lost Joseph."

Often, when we look to God for help, He answers prayer in a better manner than we hope for.

As Jacob was straining his eyes to see if his sons were returning, he saw a cloud of dust in the distance. Soon he made out the forms of his sons with the asses.

As soon as they were near enough, Benjamin jumped down from his ass and ran ahead to his father. He kissed him, crying out the wonderful news that Joseph was alive, and the ruler of all Egypt!

And then the older brothers came, with the same story.

But their father could not believe it. How could this be? Had not Joseph been dead for many years? Poor old Jacob almost fainted with excitement.

Then his sons showed him all that Joseph had sent, and told him everything that he had said to them. When Jacob saw the wagons and the twenty asses loaded with presents for him, he at last believed that Joseph was really alive, and that it was he who had sent all these good things.

"It is enough," he said. "Joseph, my son, is yet alive. I will go and see him before I die."

So Israel got ready all his family, his household goods, his flocks, and his herds to go down to Egypt to live.

How large a family do you think he had? Jacob's wives, Leah and Rachel, were both dead, but he had eleven sons. Except Benjamin, who was still very young, all his sons were married and had little children. Including the wives of his sons, there were more than sixty people in the household.

This large family, with the servants who cared for the flocks and herds, made a great train of people journeying to Egypt. The wives and the children and Israel himself rode in the wagons which Joseph had sent. The men rode on the asses, and the servants walked, driving the flocks and herds.

Soon they came to Beer-sheba, where Jacob's grandfather, Abraham, had prayed to God and planted a grove of trees, making it a place of worship. Jacob stopped to worship God there and to offer sacrifices.

There God appeared to him in the night, and said to him, "I am God, the God of thy father: fear not to go down into Egypt, for I will there make of thee a great nation. I will go down with thee into Egypt, and I will also surely bring thee up again."

This was a great comfort to Jacob, who was now such an old man that he dreaded the long journey.

PART 2 — IN THE LAND OF EGYPT

After they had traveled for a week or two through the hot, sandy desert, and were approaching the land of Egypt, Judah went ahead, to lead the way.

When Joseph heard that his father and his brothers had come, he made his chariot and horses ready to meet them.

At last he saw them coming! He made his horses go faster, because he was so impatient. Then he ran to his father, threw his arms around him, and kissed him. He was so happy, that tears rolled down his cheeks, as they sometimes do when we are very glad.

He put his head down on his father's neck and wept for a long time.

His father was just as happy as Joseph was, and he said, "Now I am ready to die, for I have seen your face, and you are yet alive."

Joseph went to tell Pharaoh that his father and his brothers had come. Jacob was brought to the palace to see the king. Pharaoh was very polite to Jacob.

When the great king saw that Jacob was a very old man, he asked him, "How old are you?"

That was the polite thing to say to very old men in those days.

Jacob answered, "*The days of the years of my pilgrimage are a hundred and thirty years. Few and evil have been the days of the years of my life, and they have not attained unto the days of the years of the life of my fathers, in the days of their pilgrimage.*"

Was not that a beautiful and dignified answer?

Then Jacob blessed Pharaoh.

Pharaoh told Joseph that his father and his brothers might have the very best part of Egypt to live in. This was the land of Goshen.

Joseph took his father and his brothers to their new home, and gave them food and everything that they needed.

"*Now the famine was very sore, so that the land of Egypt and all the land of Canaan fainted by reason of the famine.*"

As long as the people had money, Joseph sold grain out of the king's granaries to all the people of Egypt. He collected the money and gave it to Pharaoh.

As long as their money lasted, the people had plenty to eat. But by and by their money was gone. What could they do now?

They came to Joseph, saying, "Give us food, or we will die."

Joseph answered, "If your money is gone, bring your cattle and your asses, and I will give you food in exchange for your cattle."

The people sold all their cattle and their asses to Joseph for food. In exchange for the cattle, he gave them enough food to last a whole year.

They came again the next year, and said, "We are very poor. Our money is spent, and our cattle are sold to you. We have nothing left to buy food with, except our bodies and our lands. We shall die of starvation, unless you will buy us and our lands. If you will give us food, we will sell ourselves and our lands to be servants to Pharaoh."

So Joseph bought all the land of Egypt for Pharaoh, in exchange for food. All the country now belonged to Pharaoh.

Joseph was kind to the people. He did not drive a hard bargain. He gave them food to eat, and seed for their fields, and he said to them that when the better times came, and their seed grew, they should give one-fifth of their harvest to Pharaoh, and four-fifths should be their own.

The people were grateful to Joseph for making things easy for them. They said to him, "You have saved our lives by your kindness, and we shall be Pharaoh's servants, to pay for all this goodness."

At last the seven terrible years of famine were over, and once again the land of Egypt was a fertile and beautiful one. But Jacob and his sons did not go back to the land of Canaan. They were happy and prosperous in Egypt, and they stayed there.

CHAPTER 31

The Death of Jacob

GENESIS 48, 49, 50

After the children of Israel had been in Egypt for seventeen years, the time came when Jacob must die.

Someone told Joseph that his father was very ill. Joseph took his two young sons, Ephraim and Manasseh, and hurried to his father's bedside. Israel was so old that his eyes were dim with age. He said to Joseph, "Who are these?"

Joseph said, "These are my two sons whom God has given me here in Egypt."

Israel commanded, "Bring them to me, that I may bless them."

Joseph brought the two boys to his father, and Israel kissed them. Then he laid his hands on their heads and said, "I thought that I would never see you again, but now God has been so good to me that he has even let me see your children."

Jacob blessed them and said, "God, before whom my fathers Abraham and Isaac did walk, the God who fed me all my life long unto this day, the Angel who redeemed me from all evil, bless the lads. Let my name be named on them, and the name of my fathers Abraham and Isaac, and let them grow into a multitude in the midst of the earth."

Old father Jacob knew that his time had come. He called all his twelve sons to his bedside to give them a blessing before he died.

All his sons stood around him to hear his last words.

Reuben and Simeon did not receive good blessings, but when Israel came to Judah, he gave him the promise of great things. He said that from Judah's children all the kings of the children of Israel would come, and at last the greatest ruler of the Jewish people would be one of Judah's children. That one was Jesus Christ. This prophecy of Jacob's is a most important one, because in it Christ is promised.

After he had finished blessing his children, he expressed a last wish to be buried in the land of Canaan, in the field of Machpelah where his father and grandfather were buried.

When Israel had said all these things, his spirit passed away to God.

When Joseph saw that his dear father was dead, he put his face down on his father's face, kissed him several times, and cried.

Then Joseph commanded the doctors to embalm his father's body. This was never done to common people, but only to kings and great men.

We today do not know how to embalm. In some way the Egyptians wrapped cloths dipped in spices around dead bodies, so that they would not decay, though they might dry up. Bodies treated in this way are called mummies. People who have been digging in the sands of Egypt have found old coffins containing mummies which were buried more than two thousand years ago.

To honor Joseph, the whole land of Egypt mourned for Israel for seventy days.

He had said to his sons before he died, "Do not bury me in Egypt, but take my body back to the land of Canaan, and bury me with my fathers Abraham and Isaac."

Joseph asked Pharaoh, "I beg you to allow me to take my father's body back to the land of Canaan, for my father made me swear a solemn oath to bury him there." Pharaoh gave him permission to go.

Joseph made ready to go to Canaan with his father's body. Of course, his eleven brothers went with him. They did not go alone, for the Egyptians wanted to show honor to Joseph. Therefore all the servants of Pharaoh and all the elders of the land of Egypt went along with fine chariots and horsemen.

All the people of the land of Canaan looked in wonder at the grand funeral procession as it went along.

After Joseph and his brothers had buried their father in the Cave of Machpelah, they all returned to Egypt, where they had left their wives and children.

Now that their father was dead, Joseph's brothers were very much afraid that Joseph would no longer be kind to them. They thought that he might at last punish them for selling him to be a slave.

One day they came to Joseph, saying, "Our father, before he died, told us to come and beg you to forgive us for all the wickedness that we did to you when you were a boy." And they fell down on their faces before Joseph.

Joseph's eyes filled with tears. He spoke kindly to them. "Do not be afraid. You meant to do me harm, but God meant it for good. It was God who sent me here to save many people from starving. Do not be afraid, for I will take care of you and your little ones."

Joseph and his brothers lived in Egypt all the rest of their lives. After some time, Joseph's two boys were married. They had children, and Joseph had the pleasure of playing with his own grandchildren, and with some of his great-grandchildren, for he lived to be an old man.

Before he died, Joseph said to the children of Israel, "I am going to die, but God will surely bring you out of this land to the land of Canaan again. When you go, I want you to carry my bones with you, and to bury them in the land of Canaan." He made them swear a solemn oath that they would certainly do this.

Joseph was a hundred ten years old when he died. And they embalmed his body, and put it in a coffin in Egypt.

CHAPTER 32

Moses

Exodus 1, 2

Part 1 — The Israelite Slaves

The children of Israel were now settled in the land of Egypt. They lived there for many many years.

Joseph and all his brothers died. Another generation grew up and died, and another, and another. The king who knew Joseph, died, and he was followed by another Pharaoh; and he, by another. For the Egyptians called all their kings *Pharaoh*.

God gave many children to the Israelites so that as the years passed by they became a mighty nation. The land of Egypt held two different races of people — the Israelites and the Egyptians.

After four hundred years in the land of Egypt, the Israelites had grown to be a nation of three million people. They had almost forgotten that they had ever lived in another land. They had almost forgotten about Joseph, and how he had saved the land of Egypt from starvation at the time of the terrible famine when the Israelites had first come to Egypt. It was not strange that they had almost forgotten these things, for that time was as far away from them as the time of Columbus is far from us.

But they had not quite forgotten. The mothers still told their children bedtime stories of the boy Joseph who was sold into slavery by his cruel brothers, and of his wonderful rise to power, till he was next in power to Pharaoh himself. The fathers still told their sons about Abraham, Isaac, and Jacob — how holy they had been, and how God Himself had often spoken to them. They still told their sons that Egypt was not their true country, but that God had long ago promised to give the land of Canaan to them.

As one Pharaoh after another reigned, the Egyptians forgot at last who Joseph was, and what he had done for the people of Egypt in the time of the terrible famine.

There arose a Pharaoh who knew nothing about Joseph. This new king saw the mighty nation of the Israelites living in the land of Egypt, right among the Egyptians.

He did not like it. These people, though they were not Egyptians, lived on some of the best land of Egypt. He said to his people:

"Behold, the people of the children of Israel are more and mightier than we are. If there should be a war, they might join with our enemies, and fight against us. We must do something to prevent this."

He made the children of Israel work hard. Pharaoh was building two treasure cities, called Pithom and Rameses, and he made the Israelites work on these cities as slaves. He set taskmasters over the Israelites, with long whips in their hands. If they saw a man who was not working hard enough, they brought the cruel whip down on his back. The Israelites were made to do all sorts of hard work.

But the more the Egyptians afflicted them, the more they multiplied and grew.

When Pharaoh saw this, he thought of a still more harsh way to prevent their becoming stronger. He commanded that whenever a little boy baby was born in any Israelite home, the people must throw it into the river. The little girl babies might live, because they could not grow up to be soldiers who might fight against the Egyptians.

PART 2 — A STRANGE CRADLE

Now in these evil days, a beautiful boy baby was born to a father and mother among the Israelites. He was a very fine baby, strong and well. His mother made up her mind to hide him, for she knew the Egyptian soldiers would come and throw him into the Nile river. So she told no one that she had a new baby. She hid him where none of the neighbors would see him when they came to call. The minute he began to cry, she hushed him up very quickly.

But when he was three months old she could not hide him any longer for he cried so loudly that people could hear him even when they were outside the house.

She made a little boat of reeds, which she covered on the outside with tar to stop up the cracks and to keep the water out. She lined it with a soft cloth, and put the baby in it. She carried the basket-boat down to the river-side, and laid it gently in the reeds of bulrushes that grew near the river's bank.

Then the mother went away, for she did not dare to stay there. She feared that someone would see her, and suspect that she had a baby hidden there. The baby had a sister named Miriam, who was about twelve years old. The mother told Miriam to stand at a little distance, and to watch what happened to the baby.

Pharaoh's daughter used to go down to the river to bathe. She went to the river on that very day. While the princess was bathing, she saw the little basket among the bulrushes. She had her maid bring it to her. When she had opened it, she saw the beautiful baby, who began to cry.

Pharaoh's daughter knew at once that it was one of the Hebrew babies. She thought what a shame it would be to drown such a beautiful child. All her maids clustered around and looked at the baby. When he began to cry, they lifted him up out of the basket, cuddled him in their arms, and tried to soothe him.

The princess took him in her arms. The baby soon stopped crying, and smiled up into her face. When she saw that, she loved him, and determined to keep him for her own son.

All this time, Miriam had been watching from the bulrushes. When she saw the princess take the baby in her arms, and pet him, she ran out and asked the princess, "Shall I go and call one of the Hebrew women to nurse the baby for you?"

"Yes, go," answered the princess.

Little Miriam ran home very quickly. How happy the mother was! Her baby was safe! She hurried to the princess, who said to her, "I have found this child in the bulrushes, and I am going to adopt him. Will you take him home and nurse him for me? I will pay you for it."

So the mother carried home her baby, and took care of him for Pharaoh's daughter.

The princess had some silken and linen clothes made for him such as kings' sons wear. Every week his mother took him to Pharaoh's palace, so that the princess might see him. The princess gave him beautiful gold and silver toys, and everything that a little prince might like to have.

Although he was often taken to the palace, he lived with his mother until he was five or six years old. He played with his brother, Aaron, who was three years older than he, and with Miriam.

At last he went to live with the princess at the palace. She hired the finest teachers in the land to teach him all the wisdom and learning of the Egyptians. Since he was a prince, he must be a wise man. She named him Moses, which means *drawn out,* for she had drawn him out of the water.

Moses lived with the princess until he was forty years old. Before he went to live at Pharaoh's palace, his mother had very carefully taught him about the true God, for the Egyptians worshipped idols.

She also had taught him about Abraham, Isaac, and Jacob. She said, "You must remember that even though you are brought up to be the son of Pharaoh's daughter, you are really an Israelite, and not an Egyptian."

It was a very good thing that Moses was taught all the learning of the Egyptians. God had a great work for Moses to do when he was a man, which he could not do if he were not wise. God was already planning Moses' life.

Part 3 — A Flight Into The Desert

One day, when Moses had grown to be a man, he went out to the place where the Israelites were working. There he saw an Egyptian cruelly beat a Hebrew slave. (The Israelites were often called Hebrews.)

Seeing the Egyptian beat the Hebrew, Moses was angry. He looked this way and that. He did not see anyone else near. Then he killed the Egyptian and hid his body in the sand.

The next day he went out again to the place where the Hebrews were working. Two Hebrews were fighting with each other, and one was beating the other. He said to the man who was hurting the other, "Why do you hurt him?"

The man answered roughly, "Who made you a judge over us? Do you intend to kill me, as you killed the Egyptian?"

Moses was very much frightened, for he had thought that nobody knew anything about his killing the Egyptian. When Pharaoh heard about it, he was so angry that he wanted to put Moses to death. Moses found out about this, and ran away for his life, far away into a desert.

At last he came to the land of Midian, which was so far away from Egypt that he knew Pharaoh could not find him. It was a hot, dry country. Moses sat down by a well to rest.

Now, in that country lived a man named Jethro, who was the priest of Midian. He had seven daughters. They watched the sheep in the fields, for their father had large flocks.

These young girls brought their sheep to the well, and let down their pitchers to draw up water for the sheep. They poured the water into a trough, so that the sheep could drink.

But some rough country boys came around, who were also shepherds. They pushed the girls rudely away, and began to get water for their own sheep. When Moses saw how rough they were to the young girls, he helped the girls to draw up water and to water their sheep.

When the girls came home, their father said to them, "How is it that you have come home so soon today?"

They answered, "There was a very kind man there, an Egyptian. He drove away the rough shepherds, and he helped us to draw water and to water our sheep."

Their father Jethro said to them, "But why did you not bring him home with you, if he was so kind? Go back and invite him to supper."

So the girls went back to the well, and invited Moses to come and eat supper with them. Moses came, and he liked the family so much that he stayed with them. After a while, he married one of the girls.

By and by, he had a little son, whom he named Gershom, which means *a stranger here.* Soon after that, he had another little son. He named him Eliezer, which means *God is a help;* for he said, "God has helped me when Pharaoh wanted to kill me."

Moses kept the sheep of Jethro, his father-in-law.

CHAPTER 33

God Chooses Moses

Exodus 3, 4, 5, 7

Part 1 — The Burning Bush

Moses was no longer an Egyptian prince, dressing in fine clothes and living in a fine palace, with many servants to wait on him.

For many years he was a shepherd, wandering in the lonely desert from one green place to another, and sleeping under the stars at night. It was a very lonely life, for in that desert country there is very little grass, and he often had to lead his flock far away from home to find enough grass for it to eat.

It is sometimes a good thing for people to be all alone by themselves. It gives them time to think about God.

One day, Moses saw a strange sight in the desert. A bush was on fire. Moses watched it a long time, but the bush did not burn up, although it kept on burning.

This was so queer that Moses thought he would go over to the bush and find out, if he could, how it could keep on burning without being destroyed.

When Moses came near to the bush, something still more strange happened. A voice called to him out of the bush.

Someone said, "Moses! Moses!"

Moses was surprised, but he answered, "Here I am."

The voice said, "Do not come any nearer. Take off your shoes, for the place on which you are standing is holy ground."

In that country it still is the custom for people going into a church or into any other holy place to take off their shoes, instead of taking off their hats, as we do. So Moses took off his shoes.

It was God who was speaking in that bush.

Moses and Aaron said to the people, "Every family must take a lamb."

Exodus 12

"We are free! We are free!" they shouted to each other. Exodus 14

Moses wrote down in a book all that the Lord had said to him. Exodus 24

*The cover of the ark was made of pure gold,
and on it were two golden cherubim.*　　Exodus 37

A long, long time had passed since God had spoken to any man. The last time He had spoken to man was when He had told Jacob not to be afraid to go down to Egypt.

How many years do you think had passed since then? More than four hundred years!

In those days the Bible had not yet been written. Fathers and mothers had to tell their children about God, and how He had spoken to their fathers, Abraham, and Isaac, and Jacob. They said to their children, "You must remember that we are not like the Egyptians, who worship the sun and all kinds of animals. We are Israelites, and our God is the great God who made Heaven and earth. We must not pray to idols."

But it was so long since God had spoken to them, and they had had to work so hard in Egypt, that they had almost forgotten that they really had a God of their own.

Naturally, Moses was astonished to hear Him speak out of the burning bush.

God told him that He had seen the trouble of the Israelites and heard their cries, and was going to deliver them through the hand of Moses.

But Moses drew back. Although it was forty years since he had left Egypt, and surely Pharaoh would have forgotten about his killing the Egyptian, yet he feared to go back.

So he said to God, "Who am I, that I should go to Pharaoh, and that I should bring the children of Israel out of the land of Egypt?"

God promised "I will certainly be with you."

Moses knew that the children of Israel had almost forgotten that they had a God; so he answered, "But when I come to the children of Israel and say to them, 'The God of your fathers has sent me to you,' they will ask, 'Which God are you talking about?' What shall I say to them?"

God said to Moses, "Tell the children of Israel, ' I AM has sent me to you, the God of your fathers, the God of Abraham, the God of Isaac, and the God of Jacob:' this is my name forever."

Then He told Moses to go down to Egypt and gather the chief men of the children of Israel and tell them what God had said. They would believe his words. Then he and the elders must go to Pharaoh and ask him to let the children of Israel make a three days' journey into the Wilderness.

God told Moses that at first Pharaoh would not let them go. God would punish him for his refusal, and then the king would let the people be free. The Lord promised that when the Israelites should leave Egypt they would take with them the fine clothes of the Egyptians and their richest jewels of gold and silver.

"But," said Moses, "they will not believe me, nor listen to what I say. They will not believe that the Lord has appeared to me."

Then the Lord asked "What are you holding in your hand?"

"A rod," answered Moses.

"Throw it on the ground," said the Lord.

Moses threw it on the ground. It turned into a big snake. Moses was afraid of the snake and ran away from it.

But the Lord said, "Take hold of its tail."

Moses believed that if the Lord could turn a rod into a snake, He could also keep it from biting him. He did as God told him to do. He ran after the snake and caught it by the tail. It turned back into a rod again.

Then God said, "Put your hand into your bosom."

Moses put his hand into his bosom, and when he drew it out, it was as white as snow· It looked like a dead man's hand. Moses knew that his hand had a dreadful disease called *leprosy*, which cannot be cured.

He looked at his hand with horror.

But God said to him, "Put your hand into your bosom again."

Moses did so, and when he drew it out, it was no longer deadly white with leprosy, but brown and healthy, just as it had been before.

"Now," said the Lord, "I have given you two signs. If they do not believe the first sign, they will believe the second one. If they do not believe that, take some river water and pour it out upon the dry land, and it shall become blood upon the dry land."

But Moses still did not want to go. He objected, "O my Lord, I cannot speak well. I am slow of speech."

The Lord asked, "Who made man's mouth? Was it not I, the Lord? I will help you to speak."

Still Moses hesitated. He said, "O my Lord, please send someone else."

But God wanted Moses to go. He said, "I know that your brother Aaron can speak. You must tell him what I have said. Let him do the speaking to the people."

Moses finally saw that the commandments of God must be obeyed.

PART 2 — THE BEGINNING OF THE TASK

Moses went to his father-in-law Jethro, and said to him, "I want to go back to Egypt to visit my family, and see if they are still living."

Jethro replied, "Go in peace."

In the meanwhile, God had also told Moses that he need not be afraid to go, for the Pharaoh who wanted to kill him was now dead.

God also commanded Aaron, Moses' brother, to go into the desert to meet Moses. It was many, many years since Aaron had seen his brother Moses. When he met him in the desert, he was very glad to see him, and he kissed him.

Then Moses told Aaron all the things that God had said to him, and also about the signs of the snake and the leprosy.

At last Moses and Aaron reached Egypt. There they gathered together the chief men of the children of Israel. Moses told them what God had said to him, and showed them the signs of the snake and the leprosy.

The people were very glad to hear Moses' words, and to know that God was going to deliver them out of the cruel slavery in Egypt; and that He was going to take them back to the country which they had come from, which He had promised to give to the children of Abraham, although none of them had seen it.

After Moses and Aaron had talked to the elders of the children of Israel, they went to the palace of Pharaoh.

It was the palace where Moses had grown up, but the same king was no longer there.

Moses and Aaron went into the palace, and said to the king, "The Lord God of the Hebrews says, 'Let my people go, that they may hold a feast for Me in the wilderness.'"

Pharaoh looked with scorn at these two Israelites who had dared to come into his palace to ask such a thing as that.

He answered coldly, "And who is the Lord, if I may ask? I never heard of such a God as the Lord, and I certainly will not let Israel go."

They replied, "The God of the Israelites has told us to go. Let us go, we pray, for three days into the desert, to worship the Lord our God, or He may be angry with us."

The king continued to speak very proudly to them. He said, "Moses and Aaron, you go back to your work, instead of talking to me about going into the desert. Here you are, keeping all the people from their work."

Pharaoh would not listen to Moses and Aaron. He called the task-masters and said to them, "Make these people work harder. They are lazy, and that is the reason why they say, 'Let us go and worship our God.'"

Now the bricks that the Israelites made were of clay. They had to make the clay wet, then shape it into bricks, then dry these in the hot Egyptian sun, till they became hard.

But the Egyptian clay was not very good, and it would not stick together well. The Israelites had to mix straw with it to make it hold its shape. The task-masters supplied the workers with straw to put into their bricks.

Now Pharaoh, to make the work harder, told the task-masters not to give the workers straw, but to make them go out into the fields and find their own straw. Yet they must make the same number of bricks as always.

Of course the people could not do this. The task-masters beat them, asking, "Why have you not made as many bricks today as you used to?"

When things were very hard, the workers went to Moses and Aaron. "See now," they complained, "what you have done. You have made Pharaoh hate us, and he is killing us with work."

So Moses said to the Lord, "Why did You send me down here to Egypt? It has only done harm, and made Pharaoh angry with the people. You have not delivered them as You promised."

The Lord answered that soon Pharaoh would be so anxious for the Israelites to go that he would drive them out of the land. Jehovah had not forgotten His promise to bring the Israelites to the land He had promised to Abraham, Isaac, and Jacob.

So Moses told the children of Israel what God had said. But the people were suffering so much that they did not listen to him.

And God said that Moses must tell Pharaoh that he must let the children of Israel go out of his land.

Moses answered, "The children of Israel would not listen to me. Would Pharaoh listen, if the Israelites would not?"

The Lord said, "No, Pharaoh will not listen — not till I do great wonders in the land of Egypt, so that the Egyptians also shall know that I am the Lord, the great God."

God made all the nations of the earth, and He wanted all people to know about Him and to worship Him.

Moses and Aaron went to Pharaoh, and Aaron cast down Moses' rod before Pharaoh. It became a serpent. Pharaoh called his wise men and magicians, and every one of them cast down his rod, and it became a serpent also. But Moses' serpent swallowed all the others! Still Pharaoh paid no attention to Moses and his miracle. He thought that it was a strange thing, but since his magicians could make their rods turn into snakes too, he would not believe Moses. In those olden times, the magicians could do clever tricks, but they could not perform real miracles, as Moses did.

CHAPTER 34

A Stubborn King

EXODUS 7, 8, 9, 10, 11

PART 1 — GOD SENDS PLAGUES

God told Moses that Pharaoh's heart was hardened, and that he would not let the people go.

He told Moses to go to meet Pharaoh at the river the next morning, and warn him to obey God. If he would not obey, God would turn all the water of the river into blood.

Moses and Aaron did as God had commanded, telling the king what God would do if he did not let the people go.

You must remember that Pharaoh had never heard anything about the true God who had made heaven and earth and all things.

At that time everybody was heathen, except the Hebrews. God had taught Abraham about Himself, but all the nations round about had forgotten long ago that there was only one true and living God who had created all things.

They had made many gods for themselves. The Babylonians had a number of gods, and the Canaanites had other gods, and the Egyptians had theirs. In those days it was thought that each nation's gods were good for that nation only.

Pharaoh thought, naturally, that the god of a slave people like the Hebrews could not be very powerful. He scorned them and their threats. The great Pharaoh would not listen to the commands of the God of a people who were his slaves.

So Aaron took Moses' rod and stretched out his arm over the Nile river, and over all the little rivers and lakes.

All the water turned into blood. All the fish in the river died, and a bad smell came up from the river, because of the number of dead fish.

The magicians of Egypt did the same with their enchantments. Perhaps they dropped a little red powder into some water to make it look like blood.

And so Pharaoh did not pay any attention to Moses and Aaron. He just turned around and walked into his house.

The river water remained blood for a whole week. The Egyptian people did not dare drink it, since the water had killed the fish, and they themselves almost died of thirst. They dug wells near the river so that they could get a little good water.

The Lord commanded Moses to go to Pharaoh again, and say to him that if he would not let the people go, God would fill all the land with frogs.

Moses went to Pharaoh, but the king did not listen to him.

The Lord commanded Moses to tell Aaron to stretch out his hand over the rivers, and the frogs would come.

Aaron stretched out his hand, and great armies of frogs came out of the river. They marched right up into the houses and into the king's palace, until the houses were filled with loathsome frogs.

They climbed on the chairs, so that when the people wanted to sit down, they first had to knock off frogs. The frogs climbed up on the beds, crawled under the pillows, and crept between the sheets. When anybody wanted to go to bed, he first had to shake out the frogs. It was of no use, for just as soon as he was in bed, he would feel the slimy things crawling over his face.

It was almost impossible to walk without stepping on frogs. They hopped into the food and drink, and into the dough as the women were making bread.

The magicians also produced some frogs, but that was only a trick. They could easily have picked up a few of them and put them into their pockets, and then pretended that they had made them. Today we know that no man can create even one living frog. Only God can create life.

After a few days of this frog plague, even Pharaoh could stand it no longer.

He sent for Moses and Aaron. He said to them, "Pray to the Lord that He will take away the frogs, and I will let the people go."

He began to see that even if the God of the Hebrews were the God of a slave people, He was very powerful.

So Moses and Aaron cried to God to take away the frogs.

The Lord did so. The frogs died, all over Egypt. There were dead frogs everywhere — on the floors, in the beds, on the tables, all over the ground. Oh, it was horrible!

The people gathered them up in heaps and dug holes to bury them, because an evil smell rose from the dead frogs.

But when Pharaoh saw that the frogs were gone, he hardened his heart and would not let the children of Israel go.

The Lord commanded Moses, "Tell Aaron to stretch out his rod, and to strike the dust of the ground, and it shall become lice upon man and beast."

Aaron did so, and soon every person and every animal was covered with crawling, biting lice.

The people were almost crazy with the itching of their bodies. They scratched themselves until the blood came, but the lice were so thick that they could not get rid of them.

The magicians tried to produce lice, but they could not do it. They said to Pharaoh, "This is God's doing."

But Pharaoh was a very obstinate man. He paid no attention to all these God-sent warnings.

PART 2 — MORE EVILS VISIT EGYPT

Again God told Moses to rise up early in the morning and go to meet Pharaoh at the river, saying to him,

"Thus saith the Lord, 'Let My people go, that they may serve Me. If you will not let them go, I will send swarms of flies upon you. They shall fill your houses, and even the ground shall be covered with them. But I will put a difference between My people and the Egyptians. There shall be no flies in the houses of the Israelites. And so you shall know that I am the Lord, and that I can do what I will on the earth.' "

The next day the Lord sent great swarms of flies into the house of Pharaoh, and into all the land of Egypt.

Everything and everybody were covered with flies. They flew into the people's faces, into their ears and eyes and noses, and even into their mouths.

Their soup was full of flies, and their bread and meat were black with them.

Even Pharaoh could stand it no longer. Again he called for Moses and Aaron and said to them:

"Sacrifice to your God right here in Egypt. There is no need for you to go out in the wilderness."

But Moses said, "Oh, no! We can't do that! When we sacrifice, we kill sheep and oxen. The Egyptians worship these animals, and if they see us killing them, they will stone us. We will go a three days' journey into the wilderness, and there we will sacrifice as our God tells us to do."

"Well," said Pharaoh, "I will let you go, but do not go very far away."

"Very well," agreed Moses. "I shall pray the Lord to take away the flies tomorrow. But do not let Pharaoh tell lies any more, changing his mind about letting the people go."

Moses went away from Pharaoh, and prayed to God to take away the flies. God took them away, so that not one was left.

But Pharaoh broke his promise again, and would not let the people go.

And the Lord told Moses to go to Pharaoh's palace and say to him that if he should still refuse to let the people go God would send a dreadful sickness upon all Egypt's animals, and many of them should die. But He would not send any sickness upon the cattle of the Israelites, and none of them should die.

The next day the Lord sent the sickness to the animals. Almost all of the cattle of Egypt died.

Pharaoh sent some of his servants to find out if any of the cattle of the children of Israel had died. He found that not one of their cattle lay dead.

But Pharaoh hardened his heart again, and he would not let the children of Israel go.

And the Lord told Moses and Aaron to take some handfuls of ashes from the furnace, and throw them into the air in the sight of Pharaoh.

Moses and Aaron did as God had told them. Soon everybody in Egypt was covered with sore boils which made the people sick and miserable.

The magicians could not even try their tricks, because they were so sick that they could not stand up.

Again the Lord told Moses to warn the king to let God's people go to serve Him. If he would not let them go, God would send all His plagues, so that Pharaoh might know there is no other God like Him in all the earth.

But Pharaoh was a cruel man. Even though all his people were suffering, he would not give in.

God let Pharaoh be so stubborn so that all the people of the earth might see the power of the Lord, and worship Him.

Moses told Pharaoh this. Then he said that if he should refuse to let the people go, God would send a terrible rain of hail the next day. He warned the king to send his cattle and servants into barns, or they would be killed by the hail.

All the servants of Pharaoh heard this warning, too. They were not as stubborn as Pharaoh. They began to think that the God of the Hebrews was a very great God, much more powerful than their idols of wood and stone, which could not do anything at all.

The news that the God of the Hebrews was going to send a storm of hail soon spread over all the land of Egypt. All the people who feared the Lord made their servants and animals run under shelter. Those who did not fear the Lord left their servants and animals out in the fields.

Then the Lord sent a most fearful storm. Peal after peal of terrific thunder sounded. Rain came down in torrents, with hail stones so big that if one struck a man or beast, he was instantly killed. Lightning flashed across the sky, and great balls of fire ran along the ground. All the trees were broken in pieces with the terrible force of the storm.

There had never been such a storm in Egypt before. It did not stop in half an hour, or an hour, as our storms generally do. It kept on and on without stopping.

But in the land of Goshen, where the children of Israel were, there was no hail at all.

The Egyptians were almost dying with fear as they crouched in their houses, and even Pharaoh was terrified. This was far worse than flies, or sick animals. This surely came from Almighty God.

At last even Pharaoh's hard heart gave in, and he sent for Moses and Aaron, saying, "I have sinned this time. The Lord is righteous, and I and my people are wicked.

"It is enough. Pray to the Lord that there be no more thundering and hail. Then I will let you go."

And Moses said, "As soon as I have gone out of the city, I will pray unto the Lord, and the thunder and hail will stop, so that you may know that the earth is the Lord's. But I know that you and your servants will not yet fear the Lord enough to do His will."

When Pharaoh saw that the thunder and hail were over, he and his servants immediately sinned still more. They would not let the children of Israel go.

What do you think the people of Israel, in the land of Goshen, thought of these wonders?

They had been in the heathen land of Egypt four hundred thirty years. They had almost forgotten that they had a God who was much more powerful than the heathen idols. They began to rejoice, when they saw how wonderful their own God was. They began to serve Him better.

Another reason why God did all these wonderful things was that His own people might know that He is the great God of the whole earth, and that anyone may turn towards Him and worship Him.

PART 3 — PHARAOH WILL NOT GIVE IN

The Lord commanded Moses, "Go in and talk to Pharaoh."

So Moses and Aaron came and spoke to Pharaoh in a very lordly way, saying that if he would not let the people go, the Lord would send a plague of locusts. The locusts would fill all the houses, and eat all the growing things in the fields.

Moses did not wait for Pharaoh to answer him, but turned his back. With his head high in the air, he walked out of the palace.

Pharaoh's servants said to their master, "How long shall this man torment us? Let the people go. Do you not know that Egypt is utterly ruined already?"

Pharaoh said, "Very well, then, call the man back."

Some servants ran after Moses and Aaron and told them to come back, for Pharaoh would let the people go.

When they returned, Pharaoh said to Moses and Aaron, "You may go. But which of the people do you want to go?

Moses replied, "We will go with our young and our old, with our sons and with our daughters, with our flocks and with our herds, for we want to give a feast to the Lord."

Pharaoh insisted, "No, indeed, all of you can't go! The men may go, if they want to, but the rest must stay here."

He was too proud to talk with them any longer. He turned his back, and told his servants to drive them out of the palace.

So the Lord said to Moses, "Stretch out your hand for locusts to come over the country."

Moses stretched out his hand, and the Lord brought an east wind for a whole day and a night. In the morning, the wind brought the locusts.

The locusts covered the earth, so that the people could not see the ground. They ate every green thing that the hail had left, just as God had warned.

Pharaoh called for Moses and Aaron in haste. He was very humble this time. "I have sinned against the Lord and against you. Now I pray you to forgive my sin, only this once, and entreat the Lord to take away this death."

Moses prayed to the Lord. The Lord brought a strong west wind, which carried all the locusts into the Red Sea. But still Pharaoh would not let the children of Israel go.

Once more the Lord spoke to Moses: "Stretch out your hand toward heaven, and there will be darkness over the land of Egypt — darkness so black that it may be felt, as well as seen."

Moses stretched forth his hand. There came thick darkness over all the land of Egypt.

When it is a dark night now, there is always a little light from the moon and the stars, so that we can see a little, after our eyes are used to the darkness. But this Egyptian darkness was without a single ray of light. No matter how long the people stared, they could not see anything at all.

They stayed just where they had been when the darkness came upon them. They dared not move.

After three days Pharaoh could stand it no longer. He called Moses and said to him:

"Go and serve the Lord. Take your little ones along, but leave your flocks and your herds here."

But Moses answered, "You must let us take our flocks and herds, because we need them for sacrifices and burnt offerings. Our cattle must go with us too. Not one of them shall be left behind."

Then Pharaoh became very angry. He lost his temper and shrieked, "Get out of here, and don't come back, for if you do, I will surely kill you."

Moses said, "Very well, I will not come again. Let me tell you, O Pharaoh, that the Lord will pass through Egypt, and the first-born of every family shall die, no matter who it is, from your first-born son who should sit upon your throne, to the first-born of the servant-maid who works in the mill! And I tell you, O King, there will be a great cry in Egypt — a cry greater than there has ever been before, or ever will be again. But against the children of Israel shall not even a dog move his tongue, so that you may know that the Lord makes a difference between the Egyptians and His people."

As Moses talked to Pharaoh, he became angrier. He finished by saying,

"And I tell you that I won't have to come here any more. Instead all your servants will come to me. They will bow down to me and cry, 'Get out, get out, and take all your people with you!'

"And then, O Pharaoh, *then* I will go out!"

And Moses turned his back upon Pharaoh, and stalked out of the palace.

CHAPTER 35

The Children of Israel Leave Egypt
Exodus 12

PART 1 — GETTING READY

Moses and Aaron had to hurry. A very busy time was before them. They had to get the children of Israel ready to go out of Egypt in a very short time.

It was a great task to move so many people. Preparations had to be made, for when the time came, the Egyptians would hurry them out without giving them time to get ready.

Moses and Aaron said to the elders of the people, "Let every man and woman go and ask the neighbors to give him jewels of gold and jewels of silver, and good clothes."

That was to pay for the long years when the Israelites had worked as slaves, without pay. God did not want His people to be poor. They were going into a strange land, where they would need money to buy food and other things.

Moses and Aaron said to the people, "Let every family take a lamb, and kill it in the evening. Collect the blood of the lamb in a basin, and sprinkle the two door-posts and the top post with the blood of the lamb.

"None of you may go out of the door of his house from evening till morning.

"The Lord will pass through the land in the night to smite the Egyptians. When the Lord sees the blood upon the door-posts, He will pass by your house, and will not destroy you."

Moses gave another command to the people. "After you have done this, you are to roast the lamb and eat it. You must dress yourselves ready for a journey, for you are going to leave Egypt in a great hurry. Put on your shoes and your outside coat, and fasten your belt, and have your walking stick in your hand."

The people in that hot country did not wear shoes or coats in the house. They put them on only when they were traveling. They wore a long sort of coat. When they were going to walk, they tucked it up with a belt, so that they could walk more easily.

After the people were dressed for the journey, they must mix flour and water for bread, without putting yeast in it. This mixture must be ready before they could leave Egypt.

The children of Israel went away, and did as Moses had commanded.

What a day it was for them! Getting ready to go out of Egypt!

Packing the baby's clothes in a little bundle, so one of the children could carry it on his back! Packing some of the household goods on an ass! Getting another ass ready for dear old grandmother to ride on, with one or two folded blankets for a saddle so she would be comfortable!

Each one of the children had to carry something. We can imagine the scene.

"Here, Reuben, you are the oldest — you can carry this big bundle. Let me strap it on your shoulder. That is the easiest way to carry it."

"Miriam, here are your clothes and Baby's, in this bundle. I think that won't be too heavy for you."

"Little Rachel can carry this little bundle. Come here, Rachel, and let me strap it to your shoulders, so you won't lose it."

Towards evening, all of the people killed a little lamb and let the blood drip into a basin. Then the father of each family sprinkled the door-posts and the top of the door with the blood.

When the Lord would see the blood on the door-posts, He would pass by that house.

The little lamb had died instead of the first-born.

That is why Christ is called the "Lamb of God." He died on the cross and His blood was shed, so that we could go to Heaven, instead of suffering a just punishment for sin in hell.

After all the people had killed a lamb and sprinkled its blood upon the door-posts, they quickly made ready a fire to roast the lamb, for they must eat it before they left that night.

The children of Israel had had a very busy day, but it was all over now. Everything was ready, except that the yeast was not mixed, nor the bread baked.

In the land of Goshen all was quiet that evening. They waited.

The Lord passed through the land of Egypt at midnight, and smote the first-born of the Egyptians, from the first-born of Pharaoh to the first-born of the captive that was in the prison. The first-born of all the cattle died too.

Pharaoh rose up in the night, and so did all the Egyptians; for there was not a house where there was not one dead.

A terrible shriek rose from the palace. The crown prince was dead! In fear and grief the wicked king looked at his dead son, and shriek after shriek rose from the terrified servants.

All over Egypt rose a cry, for in each house there was one dead.

But in the land of Goshen no one had died. The Lord had passed over the houses sprinkled with blood.

Pharaoh, in his terror, did not wait till morning, but he called for Moses and Aaron in the middle of the night.

He cried out, "Start right away, and get away from here. Take everything with you and go! Take your people and your flocks and your herds, and be gone, as fast as ever you can. Don't wait for anything!"

The Egyptian people ran into the Israelite houses, and yelled to them, "Go out of our land as fast as you can. Go! or we shall all be dead men. If you stay here the Lord will kill us all. Hurry! Hurry! and get out of our country!"

"But we have to bake our bread first," objected the Israelites. "Otherwise we won't have anything to eat on the way!"

"No, no, you can't wait for that. Take your dough with you and bake it on the way, when you are out of Egypt!"

So mother had to tie a cloth over the bread-pan, and take the dough with her.

They asked their neighbors, "Will you give us your jewels of gold and silver and some nice clothes, if we will go?"

"Yes, yes!" said the Egyptians, "Take everything you want!"

They brought out their most beautiful gold chains, and gold earrings, and gold bracelets, and all their silver jewelry, and all their finest clothes, and heaped them upon the Israelites.

"Here, take them all," they said, "only go! Go just as fast as you can! Don't wait a minute! We won't feel safe till you are out of our country!"

Part 2 — Good-Bye to Slavery

It was well that the Israelites had made everything ready. Now it took only a short time for the three million people to start. They were dressed for the journey, with everything packed.

And they had had a good supper. The little lamb was killed so that, by its blood, it could save the first-born. But it was the kind thought of God to tell the people to roast the lamb and eat it before they went on their long journey. None of them now would go hungry. God takes care of us, not only in big things, but in little things too.

The Bible tells us to "cast our care upon God, for He cares for us." It was God also who had told Moses to tell the people to make everything ready beforehand, so they could start quickly. Indeed, God was kindly taking care of them in every way.

Moses gave the order to form into procession, and to walk five in a row. In a short time everyone was in line.

Then Moses called out to the officers and elders, "Ready! March!" and the journey began.

Was there ever such a procession as that! Three million people by families!

Not all of them were walking. The old people and the small children had to ride.

All of the flocks and herds were in that procession too. The household goods were loaded on the asses and the camels.

They started at Rameses, in the land of Goshen. They marched on until they were out of Egypt.

Then the procession stopped. They removed folded tents from the backs of the camels and asses, and set them up. Each family gathered some twigs for a little bonfire, and made some stones very hot in the fire. Then they brushed off the ashes. They made little flat cakes of the dough they had brought with them, and laid the cakes on the hot stones, baking them that way. The dough contained no yeast, because they had had to leave so suddenly. The bread tasted more like crackers than bread. But it was very good food to the hungry Israelites, who had been walking all day.

Oh, what fun the children thought it was, to eat out of doors and to sleep on the warm sand under the tent! It seemed to them like a picnic!

There was an important thing the Israelites had taken along with them. It was Moses who had thought about it. They had the bones of Joseph with them. Joseph had been dead for three hundred years, but his body had been embalmed by the Egyptian doctors. Now at last he was to be taken back to Canaan, as he had made his children promise.

How long had the children of Israel been in the land of Egypt?

They had been there just four hundred thirty years since Jacob had come to Egypt with his family of seventy persons, besides many servants. When the hosts of the Lord marched out of Egypt, four hundred thirty years later, they were about three million strong.

By the command of God, Moses told the children of Israel something of very great importance:

"This night must never be forgotten, for in it the Lord has brought us out of Egypt.

"When this night comes around every year from now on, we must celebrate it in remembrance of the wonderful way in which the Lord brought us out of Egypt. We must kill a little lamb, and pour out its blood, and sprinkle the door-posts with the blood. We and our children and our children's children must remember that when the Lord passed through the land of Egypt to kill the first-born in every house, He passed over the houses where He saw the blood. The little lamb died instead of the first-born.

"We shall call this night each year the *Passover Night,* and we shall eat the lamb in the very same way that we have eaten it this first night — with our shoes on and our sticks in our hands, just as if we were going on a journey in a hurry. We shall eat bread without any yeast in it, just as we did this time. That will make us remember this night.

"And when our grandchildren ask us, 'What does this Passover mean?' we shall say, 'It is the Lord's Passover, to make us remember the day when He smote the Egyptians, but passed over our houses.'"

The Lord commanded the children of Israel to keep this Passover for a whole week of each year, and to eat only bread without yeast for that entire week. On the last day of that week, they were to kill the lamb and eat it.

CHAPTER 36

The End of the Egyptians

Exodus 13, 14, 15

How were the children of Israel going to find their way in the wild desert?

God went before them to lead them through the wilderness. He went before them in a pillar of cloud. At night this pillar of cloud glowed like fire. This pillar traveled in front of them, night and day, to lead them on their journey. When God wanted the people to go on, the pillar of cloud moved ahead, and when God wanted them to stop, the pillar of cloud stopped.

God told Moses to let the people march up to the Red Sea, and then to stop and pitch their tents by the shore of the Sea.

After the children of Israel had been gone from Egypt for a few days, Pharaoh began to regret that he had let them go. Who would now work for him? Who would finish building his treasure cities, if he had no slaves?

So Pharaoh had his chariot prepared, and he took all the chariots of Egypt, with horses to draw them. There was a driver in each chariot, and a captain to shoot arrows.

Then Pharaoh and his army started after the children of Israel.

The Israelites had camped on the shore of the Red Sea, as God had commanded them. They had not gone far, for most of them were walking. There were many little children with them, who could not walk fast. They had many flocks and herds with them, and they had to let the animals eat the grass as they went along.

So Pharaoh and his chariots soon came in sight of the Israelites.

The children of Israel looked behind them and saw the Egyptians coming after them. They were terrified, crying to the Lord to save them.

They complained to Moses, "Why did you ever take us out of Egypt? Didn't we tell you to let us alone? It would have been better for us to serve the Egyptians than to die here in this wilderness."

Moses knew that the people were so frightened that they did not know what they were saying.

He tried to calm them. "Don't be afraid. God will take care of you. Just stand still and see how wonderfully God will save you. The Lord will do all the fighting, and you will only have to look on.

"This is the last time you will ever see those Egyptians."

Then the Lord commanded Moses to tell the children of Israel to break up their camp and be ready to march.

The Israelites began to pack up their goods in a great hurry. They did not know where they could march, for there was the deep sea ahead of them. They could not go that way, surely. Whenever they looked back, they saw the Egyptians coming nearer and nearer, and their hearts sank with fear.

But God showed his power. In that cloudy pillar that was right in front of them there was an angel, though they could not see the angel. God told the angel to change his place, and to go behind the Israelites instead of in front of them. The angel moved the pillar of cloud behind the Israelites, between them and the Egyptians. The cloud was so thick that the Egyptians could not see the Israelites at all. But on the side of the Israelites the cloud was bright and shining. It gave light to the Israelites all that night, and made it easy for them to get ready.

Moses stretched out his hand over the Red Sea, and the Lord sent a strong east wind, which blew all night. It blew so hard that the waters were moved back and stood up just like a wall on each side, and the bottom of the sea was dry.

Moses then gave the order to march.

It was a dark night, but there was no darkness at all in the midst of the Israelites, since the bright shining cloud behind them gave them plenty of light to see where they were going. Between the walls of water the Israelites marched, until they came safely to the other shore.

The Egyptians followed after the Israelites, driving their chariots right into the path in the sea.

They thought that if the Israelites could get through safely they could follow. Besides, they could see that the bottom was quite dry.

Very early in the morning, the Lord looked at the host of the Egyptians through the pillar of fire and cloud, and the Lord made trouble for the Egyptians.

Their chariot wheels began to fall off in the soft sand, so that they had to go very slowly. It was impossible to overtake the Israelites.

They began to say, "Let us go back. We must get away from these Israelites, for the Lord is fighting for them against us."

But they were in the middle of the sea. The Israelites were safely across, on the other shore. It was morning now, and the Israelites could see the Egyptians struggling in the middle of the sea, between the walls of water.

The Lord said to Moses, "Stretch out your hand over the sea, so that the water may come back again."

Moses stretched out his hand, and the waters began to go back over the path. The Egyptians saw that water was making the sea bottom wet. "Look! Look!" they cried. "The water is coming back! We all shall be drowned!"

They turned their chariots in a hurry, and they whipped their horses to make them go faster, yelling and screaming.

It was useless. The water became deeper and deeper. It came up around their waists. It was up to their shoulders. And now a big wave came rolling along over the heads of those Egyptians, and covered them from sight.

Where the Egyptians had been before, there was only the rolling, tossing sea.

Soon the restless waves began to cast up the bodies of the drowned Egyptians. The Israelites stared at their dead enemies on the sand. The Egyptians had oppressed them for many years, but they could never harm the Israelites again.

The Israelites saw once more how wonderful, how great was their God who had brought them out of Egypt with such mighty miracles.

"We are free, we are free! The Egyptians can never, never trouble us any more!" they called out to each other.

Then Moses and the Israelites sang a beautiful song to the Lord, praising him for saving them from the Egyptians.

They were so joyous and light-hearted that they felt like dancing and singing.

Miriam, Moses' sister, took a timbrel, and began to dance and sing. All the women did the same. They shook their tinkling timbrels and sang.

"I will sing unto Jehovah, for He hath triumphed gloriously,
The horse and his rider hath He thrown into the sea."

Oh, what a happy people, singing and dancing to the Lord! They were safe now, after all those hard years of slavery!

CHAPTER 37

Israel in the Wilderness

EXODUS 15, 16, 17

PART 1 — A HEAVENLY FOOD

After this happy time, the children of Israel began their journey toward the land of Canaan.

They soon came to the sandy desert of Shur. There were enough plants here for their animals to eat, but there were no brooks or little springs where the people could get water to drink.

For three days they found no water. Everyone was becoming very thirsty.

At last they came to a place called Marah. Here, to their delight, there was fresh running water. The people hastily filled their cups and water bottles with the precious water. But when they tasted it, it was so bitter that they could not drink it.

Oh, what a disappointment!

They began to find fault with Moses, asking him, "What shall we drink?"

Moses prayed to the Lord, and God showed him a tree which he must cast into the water. Moses cut down the tree, and threw it into the water. It made the water sweet, so that the children of Israel could drink all they wanted.

Soon the children of Israel came to a lovely little oasis in the desert. It was a beautiful spot, fresh and green and shady. There were seventy tall graceful palm trees there, and there was plenty of water from twelve springs. What a comfort this oasis was, after the hot, dry, sandy desert! The Israelites camped there by the waters, staying for quite a while, resting from their journey in this oasis of Elim.

But they had to move on again. They folded up their tents, packed their belongings, and started into the desert once more.

They were in another wild, rough desert country. It was called the desert of Sin.

After they had been journeying for a month and a half, they began to find fault with Moses about their food.

They said, "We wish we had stayed in Egypt, and had died there instead of coming out into this desert! We had all the bread we wanted to eat there, and here we shall probably die of hunger."

The Lord heard their complaints and told Moses that at night He would give them meat to eat, and in the morning He would send them bread from heaven.

Just then the children of Israel noticed that the cloud, which always was before their camp, was shining with a beautiful light. It was the glory of the Lord! God had come to let the people know that He had heard their murmurings.

Towards evening, great flocks of quails flew over the camp. The people caught a great many of them, and cooked them for their supper.

The next morning the ground was covered with heavy dew which looked like frost. After the dew had passed away, the children of Israel saw small white things upon the ground.

They all came out of their tents and looked at it: "Manhu?" they asked, which means "What is it?" Since no one knew, they gave it this name, or *Manna*.

It looked like seed. They picked it up in their hands and found that it tasted good.

Moses said to them, "This is the bread which the Lord promised to send you. Gather it up, as much as you need for today. Don't keep any of it until tomorrow, for it will come every day."

They gathered up as much as they wanted for that day. The sun became hot, and melted what was left.

In spite of Moses' command, some of them did keep a part of it until the morning. When they came to look at it, it was wormy and bad-smelling. Moses was very angry with them for not obeying.

On the sixth day, Moses said to the people, "Gather twice as much today. Prepare what you need to eat today, and lay up the rest for tomorrow. Tomorrow is the Sabbath, and manna will not come on the Sabbath day."

The children of Israel had been in the heathen land of Egypt, where there was no Sabbath day. In heathen countries the people do not keep a day of rest, but work every day of the week. God wanted to teach the Israelites to keep the Sabbath holy, and not to work on that day, and so He sent no manna on the Sabbath.

But some of the people again disobeyed Moses, and did not save any manna for the Sabbath. On that morning, they went out as usual to gather manna. Of course, there was none at all upon the ground.

The Lord said to Moses, "Tell those people that they *must* obey Me."

After that, the people rested on the Sabbath.

Moses said, "The Lord wants us to fill a pot full of manna and to keep it forever, so that our children and our children's children may see the bread with which the Lord fed us on our journey through the wilderness."

They gathered a pot full of manna. God kept it from spoiling, and the children of Israel saved it for hundreds of years.

This wonderful heavenly bread tasted like honey cookies. It was white, and it looked like seed. For forty years the Lord fed the Israelites with manna, until they finally came to the land of Canaan.

PART 2 — THE FIRST BATTLE

The children of Israel moved from the wilderness of Sin, and pitched their tents in the high lands of Rephidim. They were now in a very rocky country, with mountains all around them.

Again there was no water for the people to drink. Again they scolded Moses about it. "Why did you bring us up out of Egypt?" they asked. "We and our children and our cattle will die of thirst."

By this time the children of Israel should have learned that the Lord would take care of them.

Moses cried to the Lord, "What shall I do to this people? They are almost ready to stone me."

The Lord answered that he should go to one of the rocks of the mountain and strike it with his rod, and water would come out of it.

Moses did so, and a stream of fine water poured out of the rock. Now the people could drink their fill.

In these mountains of Rephidim, there were some people called Amalekites. Do you remember that Esau married two heathen wives? The Amalekites were descendants of one of these wives of Esau.

All the time that the children of Israel had been living in Egypt, the Amalekites had been dwelling in this wild, mountainous country. They were a wandering people. When they saw the great host of Israelites come through their land, they wanted to fight. They hid behind rocks and shot arrows at the last of the great host, at those who lagged behind because they were too tired or too weak to keep up with the rest.

Moses called to him a young man named Joshua, and told him to choose some soldiers to fight with the Amalekites.

Moses took Aaron and Hur, who was probably Moses' brother-in-law, and went to the top of a hill to pray. When Moses held up his hands in prayer, the Israelites drove back the Amalekites; but if Moses dropped his hands, then the Amalekites were stronger than the Israelites. Moses tried to hold up his hands, but they became so tired that he could not keep them up, no matter how hard he tried. When Aaron and Hur saw that Moses could not keep his hands up all the time, they found a big stone for him to sit on. Aaron went on one side of him to hold up his right hand, and Hur stood on the other side to hold up his left hand.

Aaron and Hur held up Moses' hands until the sun went down and the Israelites had won the victory.

God was very angry with the Amalekites, who had attacked the Israelites. God promised that He would war with them from generation to generation.

CHAPTER 38

God Talks From Mount Sinai
EXODUS 19, 20, 24
PART 1 — THE CAMP

After the Israelites had been traveling for three months, with the pillar of cloud leading the way, they came to some very high and rugged mountains, called the mountains of Sinai. You can find these mountains on your map.

Here, in front of the mountains of Sinai, the pillar of fire stopped. The children of Israel pitched their camp in the wilderness at the bottom of the mountains of Sinai.

There were six hundred thousand tents spread out in every direction, as far as the eye could reach. Each tent had a little ground around it, so that the people could gather a few sticks and make a little fire to boil or roast their manna.

In front of the camp, the people could always see the pillar of cloud by day or the pillar of fire by night.

They stayed here almost a whole year, for God wanted to teach them many things. This was a quiet place, far away from people, where they would not be disturbed or worried by anything, and could give their whole attention to what God wanted them to do.

The people of Israel had been in the heathen land of Egypt for four hundred thirty years. In all those years, no word had come from God. They had no Bible, as we have, in which to read about God. It was no wonder that many of them had begun to worship idols.

But now God was going to teach them His law, and give them His commandments, so that they would know how to live in a way that was right and pleasing to Him.

Moses was to write this law in a book, so that it could be read at any time. That was the beginning of the Bible.

Now you see why it was so important that Moses had been adopted by Pharaoh's daughter, and taught all the wisdom and learning of the Egyptians. If he had been brought up as a little slave boy, he would never have known how to read and write.

When all the people of Israel were encamped on the plain, below the rugged mountains of Sinai, God Himself came upon the top of the mountain. He called to Moses, and Moses climbed the mountain to hear what God would say.

God promised the whole nation of Israel through Moses that, if they would obey Him they all would be His own special friends, a nation of priests, and that He would be close to every one of them.

How wonderful it would have been for them, if they had truly obeyed God. They would have been almost like the angels in Heaven, who serve God day and night.

It is true that a few people truly obeyed God, and were God's special friends. But the nation as a whole did not obey Him, though they promised many times that they would.

Then God told Moses that in three days He would speak to the people right out of Heaven, and let the children of Israel hear God speak, so that they would always believe him.

After Moses had come down from the mountain, he called the elders of the people, and told them what God had said, and they told the people. And the people answered all together, with one voice, "We will do all that the Lord has said."

Moses had to get the people ready to hear God's voice.

First of all, he must put a fence all around the holy mountain where God was. Not one person, not even a beast, was to touch the mountain. If any one did, he was to be stoned to death. All the people had to wash their clothes.

On the third day, at the sound of a trumpet, the people were to gather at the foot of the mountain to hear God speak to them.

Early on the morning of the third day, Mount Sinai was covered with thick clouds. Terrible thunderings pealed through the sky, and great streaks of lightning flashed over the heavens. The mighty mountain shook and trembled, its top covered with smoke and flames.

The mighty trumpet of God sounded through the sky. When the Israelites heard the trumpet of God calling them to come, they gathered with fear and trembling at the foot of the mountain.

Louder and louder the trumpet pealed forth, till the very heavens resounded.

God Himself spoke out of the thunder, and the lightning, and the blazing fire, to the children of men.

And God spoke all these words:

PART 2 — THE TEN COMMANDMENTS

I am Jehovah thy God, who brought thee out of the land of Egypt, out of the house of bondage.

I. Thou shalt have no other gods before Me.

II. Thou shalt not make unto thee a graven image, nor any likeness of anything that is in heaven above, or that is in the earth beneath, or that is in the water under the earth; thou shalt not bow down thyself to them, nor serve them: for I, Jehovah thy God, am a jealous God, visiting the iniquity of the fathers upon the children, upon the third and upon the fourth generation of them that hate Me; and showing loving kindness unto thousands of them that love Me and keep My commandments.

III. Thou shalt not take the name of Jehovah thy God in vain; for Jehovah will not hold him guiltless that taketh His name in vain.

IV. Remember the Sabbath day to keep it holy. Six days shalt thou labor and do all thy work; but the seventh day is a Sabbath unto Jehovah thy God; in it thou shalt not do any work, thou, nor thy son, nor thy daughter, thy manservant, nor thy maidservant, nor thy cattle, nor thy stranger that is within thy gates. For in six days Jehovah made heaven and earth, the sea, and all that in them is, and rested the seventh day; wherefore Jehovah blessed the Sabbath day and hallowed it.

V. Honor thy father and thy mother, that thy days may be long in the land which Jehovah thy God giveth thee.

VI. Thou shalt not kill.

VII. Thou shalt not commit adultery.

VIII. Thou shalt not steal.

IX. Thou shalt not bear false witness against thy neighbor.

X. Thou shalt not covet thy neighbor's house, thou shalt not covet thy neighbor's wife, nor his manservant, nor his maidservant, nor his ox, nor his ass, nor anything that is thy neighbor's.

These are the *Ten Commandments*, God's law for man.

PART 3 — GOD TALKS TO MOSES

The people saw the thunderings and the lightnings, and they trembled with fear. They pushed back from the mountain in terror.

They said to Moses, "You speak to us, and we will listen. But do not let God speak to us. We shall die if God speaks to us."

So while the people stood at a distance, Moses went up the mountain into the thick darkness to talk to God.

And the Lord spoke to Moses, telling him what to say to the children of Israel.

God promised that if the Israelites would obey Him and do all that He commanded, then He would help them against their enemies, and bring them into Canaan. He would drive out the wicked nations which now lived there and give the land to His people.

The Lord promised to protect the Israelites from diseases if they would obey Him.

He warned them that when they should enter the land of Canaan they must not make friends with the heathen people there, for fear that the Israelites, too, might become heathen, worshipping idols.

After God had finished giving Moses directions about what he should say to the people, Moses went down Mount Sinai. He told the people what God had said.

The people answered, "All that God has said we will do."

And Moses wrote down in a book all that the Lord had said to him upon the mountain. That was the beginning of the Bible.

After Moses had written what the Lord had said to him, he read it to the people.

Moses wrote the first five books of the Bible — Genesis, Exodus, Leviticus, Numbers, and Deuteronomy.

God told him how the world was made, and about all those things that happened before Moses was born. God told him exactly what to write, so that there would not be any mistakes.

These are very long books, and it must have taken Moses many long years to write them. It was a very important work, for God wanted the Bible to be written so that all the people of the world could read it, to know God's commandments, and learn about His goodness and justice and holiness.

After Moses had finished telling the children of Israel all that God had said, the Lord said to Moses that he must come upon the mountain again.

Moses said to the elders of Israel, "God has told me to come upon the mountain again, and to stay there for a long time. You are to wait for me, until I come down. I will leave Aaron and Hur with you. If you have any troubles to settle, you must go to them."

So Moses left the children of Israel, and went up the mountain till the people could see him no more. He went into the thick cloud where God showed himself.

The glory of the Lord rested upon the top of Mount Sinai, and all the people could see it. It was a shining brightness, as if the whole top of the mountain were on fire.

Moses stayed up there with God a long time. He remained there forty days and forty nights.

CHAPTER 39

The Golden Calf

EXODUS 32, 33, 34

PART 1 — ISRAEL WORSHIPS THE IDOL

God gave Moses directions about a tent-church, or Tabernacle, where the people of Israel must worship God. It had to be a tent, because the Israelites were traveling all the time. A church of wood or stone they could not take along on their journey.

Aaron was to be the minister, or high priest, of the Tabernacle.

After God had given Moses very careful directions, He gave him two tablets of stone with the Ten Commandments written upon them by the finger of God.

Moses was upon the mountain for forty days and nights. He had nothing to eat in all that time, but God kept him alive.

And what did the children of Israel do all this time?

They waited at the foot of the mountain for Moses to come down again. They waited and waited, but he did not come back.

At last, they began to think that something must have happened to him. Perhaps they would never see him again!

Instead of praying to God to keep Moses safe, and to bring him back to them again, they felt that they had no one to lead them, and no God to worship.

They came to Aaron, asking him to make them an idol for a god to lead them on the journey, for they did not know what had become of Moses.

You would expect Aaron to say, "What! make you a heathen idol! No, indeed! That would be a great sin.

"God will be very angry if you make an idol and worship it, when only a month ago He spoke to you out of Heaven, and told you that you must not make idols, nor worship them."

Was that what Aaron said to the people?

No, it was what he *ought* to have said.

What he *did* say was that they should take off their golden ear-rings, and bring them to him, and he would make them a golden idol.

The children of Israel were very fond of jewelry. They had a great deal of it, for the Egyptians had given all their beautiful jewels to the Israelites. All the men, and women, and even little boys and girls, wore beautiful rings, ear-rings, and bracelets.

They took off their golden ear-rings and brought them to Aaron. He melted them and made a calf of the gold.

Then he said to the Israelites, "This is your god, O Israel, who brought you up out of the land of Egypt!"

Aaron sinned in making the golden calf. Then he went further. He made an altar before the calf and proclaimed, "Tomorrow is a feast to the Lord."

The next day all the people rose up early. They brought oxen and sheep and killed them, burning them on the altar. Then they had a big feast. They ate and drank, and they began to dance and sing and have a good time.

In those days, all the world was filled with idolatry. People thought that they must have a god that they could see. Since they had never seen God, they made shapes according to their own ideas, and called them gods.

When a man knew that he had sinned, he brought an animal. Leviticus I

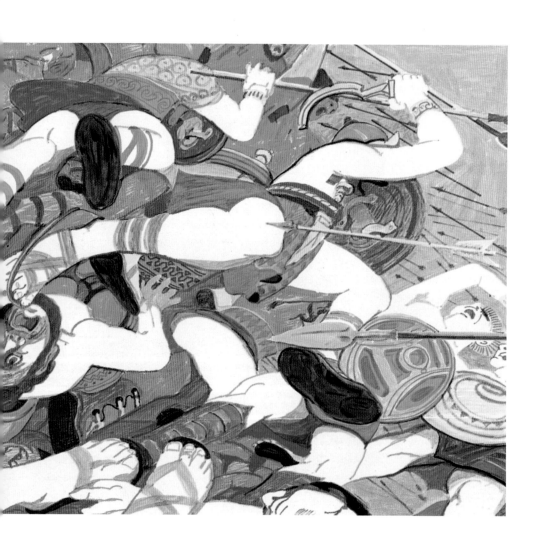

The children of Israel won a glorious victory. Numbers 21

We know better than to think that the great God could be made in any shape, for Jesus told us that God is a spirit, and that He has no body.

No one has seen God. He is so great that no one can see Him and live.

The children of Israel were disobeying God in worshipping the golden calf. They knew this, for they had heard God tell them, only a month before, not to make idols or worship them.

God saw what the children of Israel were doing, because God can see everything at all times.

Moses did not see the golden calf and the feasting, because of the thick cloud that was on the mountain.

The Lord told Moses to go down from the mountain. God told Moses the people that he had brought out of Egypt were doing wicked things. They had disobeyed the command that God had given them. They had made a calf of melted gold and were worshipping it, saying, "These are your gods, O Israel, which brought you up out of the land of Egypt."

God was very angry because of the disobedience of the Israelites. He told Moses that He would destroy them all and start a new nation of Moses and his children.

Moses was sorry that God said this. He prayed, "Oh, Lord, do not be so angry, I beseech you!

"If you kill all these people, the Egyptians will say that you have brought them out of Egypt just to kill them in the mountains. The Egyptians will say that the God of the Hebrews is not powerful enough to bring these people into the land of Canaan, and so He killed them all.

"Remember Abraham, and Isaac, and Israel. Remember that you promised them that their children should be as many as the stars of heaven. Remember that you promised to give them all the land of Canaan, to be theirs forever. O Lord, repent of this evil!"

And when Moses begged the Lord so earnestly not to destroy the children of Israel, the Lord turned away from His fierce anger.

PART 2 — THE PUNISHMENT

Moses went down the mountain. He carried the two tablets of stone in his hand. On both sides of the two tablets of stone there was writing. God had made the tablets and written the Ten Commandments on them.

We shall never know what those tablets of stone looked like. As Moses went lower down the mountain, he heard the noise of the people. He could hear them before he could see them.

He stopped and listened for a moment.

What was all that noise that he heard at the foot of the mountain? Were the people having a war? Was it the noise of a battle that he heard? It was not a battle. It sounded more like singing.

When he came a little lower, he saw the people dancing, and he saw the golden calf.

Now he knew why God was so angry.

Moses became angry, too. How could the people turn to worshipping an idol so soon after God had told them never to make one? It was most wicked! Moses' anger was hot.

In his strong feeling against the sinful Israelites, he forgot that he held in his hands the precious tablets of stone on which God had written the Ten Commandments. He flung them down the mountain, and they crashed in pieces on the rocks below.

Just as soon as Moses reached the bottom of the mountain, he took the calf and broke it in pieces. Even that was not enough. He took the pieces, and put them in a mill, and ground them into a fine powder. He threw the powder into the water and made the people drink it.

Moses ground the pieces so fine that the children of Israel could not find even a little piece to keep.

Then he turned to Aaron in his anger.

"Whatever made you do such a thing? How could you make that calf? Were the people threatening to kill you if you did not make it? You have made them commit a great sin."

Aaron said, "Do not be so angry, Moses. You know that the people are determined to have their own way. They said, 'Make us gods to go before us, for we do not know what has become of Moses.' I said to them, 'Whoever has any gold, let him give it to me.' They gave me their gold, and I melted it in the fire, and there came out this calf."

The people must be punished severely for this wickedness.

Moses knew that some of them had been leaders in this wicked thing, and that they were the ones who deserved punishment.

He knew, too, that some of the people were good, and had not wanted to join in the idolatry.

Moses stood in the gate of the camp, and he called out to the people, "Who is on the Lord's side? Those who did not want to do this, let them come and stand by me."

The whole tribe of Levi came and stood by Moses. Aaron, too, was a member of this tribe.

Moses said to them, "Every man of you take his sword, and go and kill all those bad people who persuaded Aaron to make this calf."

So the Levites took their swords, and ran among the Israelites, and killed about three thousand people who had worshipped the idol.

Then Moses said to the people, "You have been guilty of a great sin. But I will go to the Lord, and see if I can persuade God to forgive you."

Moses went up the mountain again. He prayed, saying, "Oh, this people have sinned a great sin, and have made for themselves gods of gold. If You will only forgive them—!"

Moses was so overcome by the thought of how terrible it would be if God would *not* forgive them that he could not say another word, and he stopped right there.

After a little while he went on, "But if not, then blot me out of the book which Thou hast written!"

You see that even then Moses knew that God keeps a book, in which He writes down all that we do, and keeps the names of all who try to love and obey Him.

God answered Moses, "I will blot out of my book those who have sinned against Me. Go, lead this people to Canaan. My angel shall go before you. But I will not forget to punish them for their sin."

Then God told Moses to hew two tablets of stone, like the first ones, and bring them up into the mountain on the next morning, and

He would write upon them the same words that were upon the first tablets that Moses broke.

Moses must come alone. No one might touch the mountain, and the flocks and herds might not feed upon it.

In the morning, Moses went upon the mountain all alone, with the two tablets that he had made.

Again Moses stayed up on the mountain, alone with God, for forty days and forty nights. There have been other men to whom God has spoken. But no one else in all the world has been alone with God for more than two whole months. Moses stayed forty days and nights the first time, and forty days and nights the second time.

He had nothing to eat or to drink in all that time. God kept him alive.

When God finished teaching Moses, Moses came down again from the mountain. He brought with him the two tablets of stone which he had made. God had written the Ten Commandments upon them.

Moses had been so long in God's holy presence that his face shone with a heavenly glory, though he did not know it. It was so bright that he looked like an angel.

When Aaron and the children of Israel saw him, they were afraid of him, and they did not dare to come near him.

Moses put a veil over his face. Then he told Aaron and the people to come near. He told them all that the Lord had said.

Moses kept the veil over his face while he spoke to the people. Afterwards, when he went to talk to God again, he took off the veil, for Moses spoke with God face to face.

CHAPTER 40

The Tabernacle

EXODUS 36, 37, 38

PART 1 — BUILDING GOD'S HOUSE

Moses said to the people, "We must build a tent-church for the Lord. God told me how it must be built, when I was upon the mountain.

"We shall need many things in building it. All of you who want to give the Lord something to help build the church may bring it to me.

"We shall need gold, silver, brass, and precious stones. We shall need blue and scarlet and purple cloth, and fine white linen, and rams' skins dyed red, and badger's skins. We shall need oil for the light and sweet spices for incense.

"And besides gifts, we need the help of everyone who is skillful in spinning beautiful cloth or in cutting precious stones to help make the Tabernacle."

All the people were much delighted that now they were going to have a place where they could worship God. Thy brought their treasures gladly. Soon there was much more than was needed, and Moses had to tell them not to bring any more.

God appointed two men to do the finest work. Bezaleel and Aholiab were their names. God gave them skill and wisdom to make beautiful things out of gold, to cut precious stones, to make lovely wood carvings, and to work delicate embroideries.

We know that God's ministers possess God's Spirit in a special manner. Men of genius, who are able to paint beautiful pictures and to carve beautiful statues and to play beautiful music, possess God's Spirit in a general manner.

Soon a sound of busy humming was heard throughout the camp of the Israelites, where women were spinning the curtains for God's holy Tabernacle.

How proud those skillful women were, that they had been picked out to weave these fine curtains!   They sang as they worked.

The men were busy, too, for they had to make boards for the sides of the Tabernacle. They then had to cover the boards with gold, so that when the Tabernacle was set up, it would seem to be made of gold.

Oh, it was a busy, happy time!

There was plenty of work for all the women who could spin well, because they had to make long curtains to go around the Tabernacle. Each curtain was nearly fifty feet long, and eight feet wide.

On the end of each curtain were fifty golden buttons, and on the end of the next curtain were fifty loops of blue cloth for button-holes. The curtains were buttoned together to make one long curtain.

This was to go all around the outside of the Tabernacle like a fence. It was hung upon posts made of brass. It was very beautiful, for it was blue and purple and scarlet, skillfully embroidered.

Inside the curtain stood the Tabernacle, made of boards. These boards were fifteen feet high and more than two feet wide, and they were covered with pure gold.

They stood on end, close to each other, so that they made a golden wall. Each board had two pins at the bottom which fitted into two silver sockets on the ground. The boards had golden rings into which golden poles fitted to hold the boards up straight.

This made a golden room which was forty-five feet long and eighteen feet wide. The room had only three walls. The fourth side was open, but it was covered by a beautifully embroidered curtain of blue and scarlet and purple cloth.

Inside, the golden room was divided into two parts by a curtain called the Veil. This curtain was the most beautiful of all. It was woven of blue and purple and scarlet, and embroidered with angels. It was hung on four golden pillars. The part of the Tabernacle behind the curtain was dark. It did not need any light, for a reason which I shall tell you later.

PART 2 — THE HOLY FURNITURE

The furniture, as well as the walls, had to be made of gold.

First of all, the people were to make a box or ark of wood which was to be covered over with gold, both inside and out. It was four feet long, a little more than two feet wide, and a little more than two feet high. It was open at the top, so that things could be put into it. Around the top edge was a golden crown for a border. At the four corners were four golden rings, through which two long poles could be thrust, in order that the ark might be carried on the shoulders of four men, when the Israelites were traveling. This ark was called the Ark of the Covenant.

But the most wonderful thing about the ark was its cover, which was made of solid gold. This cover was called the Mercy Seat. On the Mercy seat were two angels or cherubim, made of solid gold. One stood at each end. Their faces were turned toward each other, and they stretched out their wings above the Mercy seat, and covered it with their wings.

God told Moses to put into the Ark of the Covenant the two tablets of stone on which God had written the Ten Commandments, and also the pot of manna which God had commanded Moses to save. Now the children of Israel had a safe place for their most precious treasures.

This beautiful Ark of the Covenant was to be kept in the most sacred place of all — the golden room behind the Veil which was called the Holy of Holies. Why did it receive this name? It was called by this name because God Himself, after the Tabernacle was set up, came down into this room in the form of a brilliant light, between the cherubim on the Mercy Seat. The glory of God filled the whole room. No one was allowed to go into this holiest place, except Aaron, the high priest. Even he was allowed to enter it only once each year.

God also commanded Moses to make a table of gold, with golden rings in the corners and golden poles to go through the rings so that it might be carried easily.

This table was to stand not in the Holy of Holies, but in the outer part of the room. Every Sabbath morning twelve loaves of fresh un-leavened bread were to be put on this table by the high priest. The table was called the Table of Show Bread.

The Lord commanded Moses to have Bezaleel and Aholiab make a candlestick of pure gold. It must have seven branches, and each branch must end in a little gold cup, shaped like an almond. In the cups olive oil might be burned for light.

They made also a small altar of gold on which to burn incense made of sweet smelling spices, to spread a delicious perfume in the Tabernacle.

The Golden Candlestick and the Altar of Incense were also to be placed in the outer room. Only the Ark of the Covenant, covered with the Mercy Seat and its golden cherubim, was in the Holy of Holies.

The space in front of the Tabernacle which was enclosed by the curtain contained several other things.

First of all, there was a large altar here. It was eight feet square and four and a half feet high. This large altar was not made of gold, like the other, but of brass. On it were to be burned the burnt offerings.

There was also a large brass bowl in which Aaron and his sons had to wash their hands and feet before they could offer sacrifices to the Lord. It was called the Laver.

You can never guess how this big bowl was made. It was made of the looking-glasses of the Israelite women. At that time they did not have mirrors of glass, as we have now, but they used mirrors of fine polished brass. The women were proud to bring their brass mirrors to Moses, to make a brass basin to be used in the service of the Lord.

CHAPTER 41

Aaron and the Levites

Exodus 39

Bezaleel and Aholiab made all the beautiful things for the Tabernacle which we have just described. But this was not all they had to do. The Tabernacle was to be a church, and there must also be ministers or priests, who had to be dressed fittingly.

God appointed Aaron to be the high priest. Aaron's sons were also to be priests. After Aaron was dead, his sons were to be priests after him, and their sons after them, and so on forever.

The Tabernacle being finished, Bezaleel and Aholiab had to make some beautiful clothes for Aaron, the high priest. Aaron's sons had to have some fine clothes also, but the high priest's robes were to be much the finest.

First of all, there was a long robe made of blue cloth. Around the bottom it was bordered with little golden bells which tinkled when Aaron walked.

Over this there was another garment, called an ephod. It was woven of blue and purple and scarlet. Bezaleel and Aholiab took gold and beat it as thin as paper. Then they cut it into fine gold wires like threads. They wove these gold threads in among the purple, blue, and scarlet threads, to make the ephod still more beautiful. An embroidered belt was worn with it.

On each shoulder there was a large onyx set in gold. On each stone were engraved the names of six of the twelve tribes of Israel.

On Aaron's breast was a sparkling breastplate, hung from his shoulders by fine gold chains. The foundation was made of a square of beautifully embroidered cloth of scarlet, blue, and purple. Twelve precious stones were set in gold and then fastened to this cloth. Each stone was engraved with the name of one of the tribes of Israel.

Just think how splendid this breastplate must have been!   It was a blaze of radiance from the many-colored precious stones.

On Aaron's head was a white linen miter, a kind of hat. Over this was a golden crown, and on the crown the words, *Holiness to the Lord.*

The Levites were to help Aaron and his sons take care of the Tabernacle. There was a great deal of work to be done.   After the sacrifices, all the silver platters had to be washed, and the ashes of the burnt offerings had to be carried away. Wood had to be cut to keep the fire on the altar burning, for that fire was never allowed to go out. Since God had sent fire from heaven down upon this altar, it had to be kept burning day and night.

In case the Israelites moved from one place to another, the Tabernacle had to be taken down, packed up, and put on wagons, so that it could be carried wherever the Israelites went.

It was the duty of the Levites to do all these things. No one else was allowed to touch the Tabernacle. Only the Levites were allowed to put it up and take it down.

When they took it down, some of the Levites had charge of the curtains. Others had charge of the golden Ark, or the golden Altar, or the golden Candlestick and the silver and golden dishes. Others had charge of the pillars and sockets.

Before the Levites came in to take down the Tabernacle, if the Israelites were going to move, Aaron the high priest and his sons had to take down the holy Veil and cover the Ark of the Covenant with it. A beautiful blue cloth had to be put on top. They had to cover the Table of Show Bread with a scarlet cloth, the Candlestick with a blue cloth, and the Altar with a purple cloth.

After all these holy things were covered, the Levites were allowed to carry them.

The princes brought six covered wagons for carrying the holy things of the Tabernacle, and twelve oxen to draw the wagons.   The Levites put the things on the wagons.

But the holy Ark, and the golden Table, and the golden Candlestick and the Altar of Incense were not put on the wagons. They were carried on the shoulders of the Levites, after their shoulders had first been covered.

CHAPTER 42

The Dedication of the Tabernacle

Exodus 39, 40

After all the beautiful things for the Tabernacle had been made, Moses looked them over to see if everything had been done as the Lord had commanded. He was very much pleased with the children of Israel for working so skillfully and so faithfully, and he blessed them.

Then Moses told the people to set up the Tabernacle.

First of all, they brought the golden boards, and set them up by putting the pins in the silver sockets. They slipped the golden rods through the golden rings on the inner side, to hold the boards up straight.

Then they brought the sacred Ark of the Covenant into the back part of the golden room. They set up the four golden pillars in the middle of the room, and hung the beautiful curtain called the Veil on the hooks, so as to make a separation between the first part, called the Holy Place, and the Holy of Holies, where the Ark stood.

In the front room they placed the Altar of Incense, the golden Candlestick, and the golden Table of Show Bread.

Then they hung the long blue-scarlet-purple curtain around the Tabernacle, on brass poles, making a court or yard around the Tabernacle. In this court was placed the large brass altar on which Aaron was to burn sacrifices to the Lord. The brass Laver was in this court, too.

Was anything ever so beautiful as that golden Tabernacle, with its golden furniture, surrounded by the richly colored curtains, hanging from their shining brass poles?

Oh, how happy and proud the people were!

After the Tabernacle was set up, all the people wanted to bring gifts.

As you know, there were twelve tribes. All the people in each tribe joined together and made one fine gift. The prince of the tribe gave the gift for the Tabernacle to Moses.

God told Moses to let one prince come each day with his gift, until all of them had offered a present.

The first day the prince of the tribe of Judah came. He gave Moses a big silver platter and a silver bowl. Both of them were full of fine flour mixed with oil, for an offering to the Lord. He gave also a large golden spoon, full of sweet incense to be burned on the Altar of Incense. He brought some animals for a peace offering, too.

Besides this peace offering, the prince of the tribe of Judah brought one bullock, one ram, one young lamb, and one kid, as a burnt offering for the sins of his tribe.

And so each day a prince of one of the tribes came, offering the same gifts, until all the twelve princes had come and brought presents to the Lord.

Then Moses took some holy oil and sprinkled a little upon each piece of furniture. This was called anointing. It meant that those things were holy to the Lord, and were not to be used for any other purpose than the service of God.

Next, Moses anointed Aaron and his sons with the holy oil, to show that they had been set apart forever to be God's priests.

Last of all, Moses put the show-bread on the Table, lighted the seven lamps of the Candlestick, and burned sweet-smelling incense upon the Altar of Incense.

When everything was finished, a cloud covered the Tabernacle, and a glorious light filled the Holy of Holies. The glory of God shone forth between the golden cherubim that were over the Mercy Seat.

From this time on, the glory of the Lord always shone between the cherubim in the Holy of Holies, showing the people that God was right among them in the beautiful house that they had made for Him. The glory of the Lord was so bright that Moses was not able to go into the Holy of Holies. No man might enter there. It was God's house, and God was there.

You see, the Tabernacle was not like our churches. It was not a place where people might come to sing and pray as our churches are. It was for God.

Now that the Tabernacle was set up, God did not call Moses upon Mount Sinai when He wanted to speak to him. He talked with Moses from the Tabernacle, and told him what He wanted the children of Israel to do.

And although the people could not enter, they knew that God was there, for when the beautiful light was shining in the Holy of Holies the pillar of cloud covered the outside of the Tabernacle.

When God wanted the Israelites to journey to some other place, He took up the pillar of cloud and it moved along in front of them, leading them wherever God wanted them to go.

As long as the pillar of cloud stayed on the Tabernacle, the children of Israel rested, whether it was a day, or a month, or a year. When the cloud was taken up, they journeyed, knowing that God was leading them.

CHAPTER 43

How Israel Worshipped

LEVITICUS 1, 2, 3, 16

Because all people constantly sin against God, Aaron, the priest, was commanded to offer sacrifices of animals upon the great brass altar which was in the court outside of the golden Tabernacle.

Nowadays we do not kill animals and burn them on an altar, to take away our sins. We know that Jesus has come into the world, and that He has died on the cross to take away our sins. Jesus Himself was the great sacrifice.

But Moses and the children of Israel lived long before the time of Jesus, and they did not know about Him as we do. So God commanded that animals should be killed to take away the sins of the people.

When a man knew that he had sinned, and he felt that God was angry with him, he might bring an animal — a bullock, or a sheep, or a goat — to the Tabernacle. He then had to put his hands on the head of the animal, to show that he was putting his sins on it. The animal was then killed, and Aaron and the other priests burned it on the altar.

Thus an innocent animal, which had never done anything wrong, was killed instead of a sinful man. And God forgave the man's sin.

God did not forgive the man's sin, however, because an animal had been killed, but because Christ was going to die for sin. The dead animal was only a *sign of Christ,* who would one day die for the sins of the world. *God forgave the man's sin because in the future Christ would die for that man's sin.*

Because all men commit sin against God every day of their lives, Aaron offered sacrifice every morning and evening. A little lamb was killed every morning and evening, and its blood was poured out, and its body was burned on the altar in the court.

There were many other kinds of sacrifices. There were four kinds of animals that could be used for sacrifices — bullocks, sheep, goats, and doves and pigeons. No other animals could be used.

These offerings for sins were called *burnt offerings.*

The people might bring offerings to serve as gifts to the Lord, whenever they felt thankful to Him, or when they wanted to ask His blessing. These were called *peace offerings.*

The people must also offer oil and fine flour and cakes made without yeast. A part of these offerings was to be burned on the altar, and a part was to be given to the priests to eat.

No animal that was lame or blind or imperfect might be offered. Only the very best could be given to God.

Once a year, the Jews were to have a solemn fast day, called the Day of Atonement. On this day the children of Israel were not permitted to work, but had to rest, just as they did on the Sabbath. They had to spend the whole day thinking of their sins and being sorry for them.

This was the only day in the year on which Aaron, the high priest, was allowed to go into the inside room of the Tabernacle, the Holy of Holies, where the glory of God shone forth between the cherubim.

On this solemn day, Aaron took off his splendid garments, and put on pure white linen clothes, because he was going into the Holy of Holies to meet God.

No one might go with him.

First of all, he brought a young bullock and two young goats. He killed the bullock. Then he took a censer, which was a bowl hanging from chains, and filled it with burning coals taken from the Altar of Burnt Offering. Next he put sweet-smelling incense on the coals of fire, so that a cloud of sweet perfume was sent up.

Taking some of the blood of the bullock, he went behind the Veil into the Holy of Holies, where God showed Himself in a special way.

He swung the censer, so that the cloud of sweet-smelling incense filled the whole room. Seven times he dipped his finger into the blood of the bullock, and sprinkled the blood upon the Mercy Seat, where the cherubim were.

Then Aaron went outside and killed one of the two goats. The blood of the goat was used in the same way as the blood of the bullock. He took it behind the Veil, and sprinkled it upon the Mercy Seat.

After finishing all this, Aaron went out and laid his hands upon the head of the live goat, confessing all the sins of the children of Israel, and putting them upon the head of the goat.

Then he gave the goat to a good man, who had to take the goat far away into the wilderness. The animal was to bear the sins of the children of Israel far away into the wilderness. Then the sins would be blotted out for good.

All the time that Aaron was doing this the children of Israel were sorrowing for their sins, all day long.

When it was over, Aaron took off his holy, pure white garments, and left them in the Holy Place till the next year, when the Day of Atonement came around again.

CHAPTER 44

Israel's Feasts

LEVITICUS 23; NUMBERS 9

It was now a year since the children of Israel had left Egypt. A year had passed since that dreadful night when God had commanded them to kill a little lamb and to sprinkle its blood upon the door-posts of their houses, because in that night God would pass through the land of Egypt, and would strike the first born in every house with death.

God called Moses to come into the Tabernacle. He said to Moses:

"It is now a year since the children of Israel have come out of Egypt. Tell them to keep the Passover on the fourteenth day of this month."

The children of Israel did as they had been commanded. They kept the Passover in the wilderness of Sinai on the fourteenth day of the first month of the year.

They killed a little lamb, and the father of each household sprinkled its blood upon the door-posts of their tents. Then they ate it in a hurry, dressed for a journey, as they had eaten it on that terrible night in Egypt.

Even the little children could remember that night. After the Passover night, they ate unleavened bread for a whole week, so they would remember how they had been forced to hurry out of Egypt.

God told Moses that besides the Passover, they should have two other feasts every year. Seven weeks and one day after the Passover (fifty days after it) there should be a feast called the Feast of Weeks. At that time they should bring a gift to the Lord for having blessed them.

And late in the year, when the harvest is gathered in, they should have another feast, lasting a week, called the Feast of Tabernacles.

This Feast of Tabernacles was a very happy time. God commanded the people at this feast to cut down branches of palm trees and willow trees, and to make little arbors of them. The people were to live in these arbors for a week. They were to rejoice and be happy during this time.

How the children loved this Feast of Tabernacles! How delightful it was to live in a green arbor for a week — to sleep there, too, with only a few leaves between them and the stars! And to see, on all sides, other green arbors where their little friends were sleeping!

But while they were having such a happy time, they certainly should not forget the Lord. They had to keep the first day and the eighth day holy, so that all the people could meet together to praise God.

Aaron and the priests were to offer special sacrifices on all of these feast days. While the people were rejoicing in their arbors, the priests were offering the sacrifices brought by the people. God commanded that on these feast days, which all the men had to attend, no one might go empty-handed, but every man was to bring an offering to the Lord.

Moses had to make two beautiful silver trumpets.

Whenever the priests, the sons of Aaron, should blow on the trumpets, then all the people had to gather together at the door of the Tabernacle.

When they wanted only the princes, the heads of the tribes, to meet, then Aaron's sons blew only one trumpet.

On all the solemn feast days, and on the Sabbath mornings, the soft tones of the silver trumpets rang out on the morning air, calling the people to come and worship God.

There was one special day when these silver trumpets were to sound all day long. This was called the Day of the Blowing of Trumpets.

God made a law that after the people had settled in the land of Canaan, they should plow their land, sow their seed, and reap their harvests for six years. In the seventh year, they should not plow, sow, and reap. They should then let the land lie idle, so that it could have a rest.

If they would obey Him in this, God promised them that He would give them such a bountiful harvest in the sixth year that it would be enough for three years.

God appointed one year in every fifty to be a very special year, the Year of Jubilee. In this year, too, they should plant no crops. But the Year of Jubilee was more than a year of rest. It was a year of free, dom. I shall explain.

God promised the children of Israel that, when they came into the land of Canaan, He would give each tribe a part of the land. That part was to be theirs forever. And each tribe must divide its part into smaller pieces, a share for each family of the tribe, to belong to that family forever. Now suppose a family became very poor and had to sell the land? They could sell it. But it would be theirs again. For when the Year of Jubilee came around, the man who bought it had to give it back. It must go back to the family that first owned it. For God had given it to that family.

The Year of Jubilee was a happy year for another reason. If any Hebrew should become poor and have to work for another man, the rich man for whom he was working could not make a slave of him. He could not make him work for nothing, as slaves have to do. He had to treat him kindly. And when the Year of Jubilee came around, the poor man must be allowed to go free.

The Year of Jubilee was a great blessing to poor people. It came only once in fifty years, but the poor people looked forward to it. When it was drawing near, how happy the man was, who had had to sell his land to some rich neighbor! In the Year of Jubilee the land came back to him again. The poor man who had had to sell himself to his rich neighbor as a servant, could go back to his own family again and be a free man.

And so the poor people longed for the Year of Jubilee. When fifty years had gone by, they listened for the sound of the trumpet. The trumpet sounded out on the quiet air to "proclaim liberty throughout all the land to all the inhabitants thereof."

CHAPTER 45

God Gives Many Laws

LEVITICUS 24, 10

God gave Moses many laws besides the Ten Commandments.

There were some laws about food. The Israelites might eat the meat of cows and sheep and goats. These were called clean animals. But God said they might not eat pigs, nor camels, nor rabbits. These were called unclean animals.

God said that men may not commit murder. If a man killed another man, he must be punished with death. If a man should hurt someone, he must be punished according to the harm he did.

God very strictly commanded the people never to make an idol or image, or worship it. When He spoke to them on Mount Sinai and gave them the Ten Commandments, they heard the voice of God, but they did not see Him. God is so great that no man can see Him and live. No one may make any image and call it God.

God wanted the people to keep His Sabbath, and to do no work on His holy day.

The people had to love one another, and to be kind to the poor.

These are a few of the many laws given by God to the Israelites. God promised them that if they would obey Him and do all His commandments, He would give them a great many blessings.

God promised them that after they had taken the land of Canaan for their own, He would give them plentiful harvests. The rain would come down and water their fields whenever it was needed. All their fields and fruit trees would yield abundantly.

God would give them many children, so that their nation would grow strong.

He would give them peace, so that the nations round about them would be afraid of them and not disturb them.

God promised to keep from them the dreadful diseases that the Egyptians had had, and of which they had been afraid when they lived in Egypt.

But God said that if they would not obey His commandments, He would punish them "seven times more for their sins."

He would send them no rain, so that their grain would not grow in the fields and their fruit trees would not bear fruit. He would send burning heat, that would make the sky look like brass.

Sickness, too, would come among them.

Still God would be forgiving. He promised that if the people should be sorry for their sins when God had punished them, then He would forgive them, and be kind to them again.

CHAPTER 46

The Israelites Continue Their Journey

NUMBERS 1, 10

It was now more than a year since the children of Israel had come out of Egypt. All this time they had been in the wilderness of Sinai.

They had been very busy. First of all, God had given them the Ten Commandments and many other laws to tell them how to live. Then they had been working at their Tabernacle.

Very soon God was going to have them continue their journey, since they still had to travel far before they could reach the land of Canaan.

God told Moses that he and Aaron should number the people to find out how many men there were who could go to war. For they would meet unfriendly people, whom they would have to fight.

Only those who were twenty years or older were to be counted. Aaron's tribe, the tribe of Levi, was not counted. None of the Levites were to become soldiers. They were to help Aaron and his sons to take care of the Tabernacle.

The twelve princes of the tribes helped Moses and Aaron to number the Israelites. When the people had been counted, it was found that there were more than six hundred thousand men who were able to go to war.

One morning the Israelites saw that the pillar of cloud had moved from its place over the Tabernacle.

Oh, how excited the children were! "Look! look!" they shouted. "The cloud has moved, and we are going to travel again."

It was a busy time they had, getting all packed up and ready to go.

While everybody was hustling to get his things together, Aaron and his two sons who were left, Eleazar and Ithamar, went into the Tabernacle and covered the holy furniture so that the Levites could carry it.

Some of the Levites took down the curtains of the Tabernacle and put them on one of the wagons that the princes brought.

Other Levites took down the golden boards of the Tabernacle, and the silver sockets. They piled these away very carefully in other wagons.

Meanwhile the people were packing their clothes and taking down their tents.

They had all their animals to take with them.

"Come here, Daniel," said one of the Hebrew fathers, "I will tie a rope around the calf's neck, and you must lead him. Jacob, you are big and strong; you must carry this little lamb. It is too small to walk."

The tents had been arranged in regular order all around the Tabernacle, as God had commanded. In front, near the door, Moses and Aaron had pitched their tents. All around the Tabernacle were the Levites' tents. Farther off, in regular order, were the other tribes.

Their marching was to be as orderly as their place around the Tabernacle had been. They were to start off in a way God had told

Moses. Each tribe had a captain over it, and a flag of its own. How proud the young man was who carried the flag at the head of his tribe!

At last all was ready. The children were dressed carefully, their sandals strapped tight to their feet. Everything was packed so that it would be easy to carry. The people were eagerly waiting for the blast of the trumpet which was the signal to start.

Finally it came. Loud and long the trumpets sounded. Not a silvery, sweet tone like the one they heard on Sabbath days, but a loud alarm, a call to march.

At the first sound, the tribes on the east side of the Tabernacle started — Judah, Issachar, and Zebulun. After they were under way, the Levites came with the wagons drawn by oxen which carried the curtains of the Tabernacle and the golden boards.

Then again came the loud blast of the trumpets. This time, the tribes on the south side started. After them came more Levites, carrying the holy things of the Tabernacle on their shoulders.

When the Ark of the Covenant began to move, Moses stood up and said, "Rise up, O Jehovah, and let Thine enemies be scattered, and let them that hate Thee flee before Thee."

Then another blast sounded. This time the tribes of Ephraim, Manasseh and Benjamin started. With another call, the last three tribes began to march.

What a long procession! How fine they looked with their banners flying! In front of them went the pillar of cloud, which became a pillar of fire at night.

The children of Israel marched for three days, only stopping at nights to sleep. After three days the pillar of cloud stood still. They knew that God wanted them to stay there.

The Levites stopped the oxen, took the golden boards off the wagons, and set them up. The curtains were hung on their pillars around the Tabernacle, and the furniture was put in its place.

Then Moses stood up and said, "Return, O Jehovah, unto the ten thousands of the thousands of Israel."

CHAPTER 47

The Grumbling Israelites

NUMBERS 11, 12

The Lord kept on sending the delicious manna every morning for the children of Israel to eat.

But instead of being thankful for their blessings, they scowled and whined, saying, "We are tired of this manna. We have nothing to eat except manna all day long. We want some meat. We want some fresh vegetables, too. We remember the fish which we always ate in Egypt, and the nice fresh cucumbers, and the melons, and the leeks, and the onions, and the garlic. But now we have nothing at all except manna, and we are tired of it."

Just think how discontented they were! They could not stand to live on manna for the few weeks when they were traveling, although they knew they would soon come to a land where they could get all kinds of delicious things to eat.

Throughout the camp of Israel, people were fretting. They stood in the doors of their tents with tears rolling down their cheeks. They felt so sorry for themselves! No matter where Moses walked among the tents, he heard nothing but whining and complaining.

Moses was not happy, either. Moses was discouraged. He had so much trouble with the people. They complained so much. They never seemed to be thankful for the many blessings God sent.

Moses began to feel that it was too hard for him to have to manage all the people. Why had God chosen him to lead them to the land of their fathers? They were forever finding fault. Now they were beginning to cry, "Give us meat. We are tired of this manna." Where could Moses get meat for so many? He hadn't any meat to give them.

Poor Moses became so discouraged that at last he said he would rather die than go on.

Moses was not the only one who was weary of the grumbling. God had heard the discontented murmurs, and had seen the rebellious tears.

But God was going to help Moses. He told him to pick out seventy of the best men among the children of Israel and bring them to the door of the Tabernacle. God would put some of the spirit that was in Moses upon these men, so that they might help Moses to govern the people.

To the grumblers God would send so much meat that they would become sick of it, enough to last for a month.

Moses was so astonished that he couldn't believe God. The Israelites numbered six hundred thousand men, without the women and children. Where could so much meat come from? Must all the flocks of sheep and herds of oxen be killed?

The Lord answered Moses, "You will see whether what I have said will come to pass or not."

Moses chose the seventy men, as God had commanded. God put in them some of the spirit that was in Moses, so that they could help him rule. Moses ordered the seventy judges to judge justly and not to favor the rich more than the poor.

Then the Lord sent a wind which brought quails from the sea. Quails are big birds like chickens, and they are delicious to eat. They came in such great numbers that all the ground around the camp was covered with them. They flew so low that even the children could catch them.

The people stopped their work. All day and all night and all the next day, they did nothing but catch quails. The birds were piled high around their tents.

To keep them from spoiling, the Israelites spread the birds out on the sand. The air was so dry that the blazing sun dried them out like dried beef.

You could never guess how many quails they caught. The Bible says that even those who had caught the least, had ten homers, or eighty bushels.

Eighty bushels of quails must last a family longer than a month, for no family could eat more than half a bushel a day. How wonderfully God had provided!

God did not forget to punish those who had been rebellious and discontented. Those who had been very wicked became ill, and many of them died.

It would seem as if Moses had enough trouble with these rebellious Israelites, without having any trouble in his own family.

But his sister Miriam and his brother Aaron were jealous of him, because God had made Moses leader of the people. They wanted the people to listen to them.

Moses was a very meek man, and he did not become angry. He did not say a word to them.

But God was angry. He called Moses, Aaron, and Miriam to the Tabernacle. The Lord came down in the pillar of cloud, and the pillar stood in the door of the Tabernacle. They could not see God, but they could hear Him speak.

God told Miriam and Aaron that if there were a prophet among the children of Israel, the Lord would speak to him only in a dream or vision. With Moses, who was so true and faithful, God would not speak in a dream, but face to face. Were not Miriam and Aaron afraid to find fault with the Lord's servant?

As Aaron looked at Miriam, he was shocked to see that she was as white as snow. He knew that such a deadly whiteness could mean only one thing — that she had the most dreaded disease in the world, leprosy.

This disease was incurable. After a while, Miriam's fingers and toes would rot and drop off, and she would die. She would never again be allowed to come into the camp of the Israelites. Wherever she went among other people, she would have to cry out, "Unclean! Unclean!" Everyone would keep far away from her, for leprosy spreads from one person to another.

Aaron begged Moses to forgive them their sins, and not to let Miriam suffer this terrible punishment.

Moses cried to the Lord, "Heal her now, O God, I beseech Thee."

God spoke. "Let her be shut out from the camp seven days. After that let her be received again."

The Israelites waited for Miriam, not traveling till she was well and could go with them.

CHAPTER 48

Spies Search Out the Land

Numbers 13, 14

After Miriam's recovery the pillar of cloud lifted from the Tabernacle, and the children of Israel continued their journey until they came to the wilderness of Zin. Here they were on the very border of Canaan, the promised land.

At God's command, Moses picked out twelve of the most important men, rulers of the tribes, saying to them, "Go into the land of Canaan, and spy it out. See what the land is like — what kind of people live there, whether they are strong or weak. Find out what kind of cities there are — whether the people live in tents and roam from one place to another, or whether they have cities with strong stone walls. Find out whether the land is fertile or barren, and bring back with you some of the fruits of the land."

The twelve men started at the south. They traveled through the whole length of the land to the northern end. Then they turned around and came back again, just forty days later.

They found wonderful fruit, finer than they had ever seen before. At the brook of Eshcol they cut down a branch of a grape vine which had one bunch of grapes on it. That cluster of grapes was so large that they had to hang it on a pole on the shoulders of two men. They also found some fine figs and pomegranates.

When the people heard that the twelve spies had come back, they crowded around to hear their report.

What did the men say? "We came into the land you sent us to, and truly it flows with milk and honey! This is the fruit of it.

"But the people who live there are very strong, and the cities are large, with high stone walls around them. What is worse, we saw there the children of Anak, who are giants."

Oh, how the people's faces fell when they heard about these giants.

Caleb, who was one of the spies, said, "Let us start at once and take it, for we are well able to overcome the people of the land."

The other spies said, "No, no, we cannot conquer this country. Their people are stronger than we are."

Ten of the spies discouraged the people, saying that all the men living there were tall and strong. "We felt like grasshoppers compared to them, and we surely looked like grasshoppers to those big giants."

What a terrible disappointment!

The people began to cry and moan. All night long they moaned and complained. They blamed Moses and Aaron for bringing them all that long journey only to be disappointed at the end.

Not once did they think of asking the Lord to help them. They never even remembered that it was God who had commanded them to go out of Egypt, and who had brought them all the long way through the desert.

They said to each other, "Would that we had died in the land of Egypt! Would that we had died in this wilderness!"

In the morning they said to one another, "Let us choose a captain, and let us return to Egypt."

Moses and Aaron were struck with horror. What! Choose a captain without even asking God about it, and go back to Egypt without God! How dared they even think of such a thing? Moses and Aaron fell down on their faces and begged them not to be so wicked and foolish.

Caleb and Joshua, two of the spies, rent their clothes to show how they felt at the way the people were acting.

Their report was not like the story the others had brought back. They told the Israelites that Canaan was an exceedingly good country to live in. If the Lord loved them, He would bring them into the land and give it to them. Only they must not rebel against the Lord, or be afraid of the people of the land. Even giants could not harm them as long as the Lord was with them.

Were the people encouraged by these speeches?

No. The wicked people started to throw stones at Caleb and Joshua.

God heard the children of Israel crying in their tents, "Would that we had died in Egypt. Would that we had died in this wilderness." He saw them take up stones against Caleb and Joshua. He was very angry. All at once, God came down into the Tabernacle. His glory shone forth over the Mercy Seat.

This was not the pillar of fire that they saw every night. It was the presence of God shining forth in His terrible anger.

God spoke to Moses. The people still did not believe Him in spite of all the wonderful signs He had shown them. So again God threatened to destroy them and make of Moses a nation greater than they.

But Moses did not care for his own glory. If God should destroy the Israelites, then the Egyptians would hear it and would tell it to the people of Canaan, he said. They would say, "The Lord was not strong enough to bring them into the land that He promised to give them; so He has killed them in the wilderness."

Moses prayed God to forgive the people in His great mercy, as He had forgiven them so many times before, even from the time they had come out of Egypt.

When Moses so humbly pleaded with God to forgive the people their great sin, God answered that He would forgive them. But all the people who had seen God's glory and the miracles which He did in Egypt, and had rebelled against Him, would never see the land which God had promised to their fathers.

Only Caleb and Joshua should ever see that beautiful land, for they had followed God.

As for the rest, who had murmured against God, they must turn about and go back into the wilderness. There they must wander for forty years till every single one of them had died. Only then would God bring their children into the good land promised to Abraham, Isaac, and Jacob.

God punished the ten spies who had told the children of Israel that they could not take the land. He sent to them a plague so terrible that in a few hours they were dead. But Caleb and Joshua were not sick at all.

CHAPTER 49

The Rebellious Israelites Turn Back

NUMBERS 14, 15, 16, 26

PART 1 — A DEFEAT AND A MUTINY

Moses told the people what God had said — that because they had doubted Him they would never see the promised land.

Oh, how the people mourned when they heard the dreadful news!

Must they turn around and go back into the dreary desert that they hated so much? Would they never see the promised land after this hard journey?

You could hear the people sobbing in their tents all night. In the morning they all got up early. They said to Moses, "We have changed our minds. We will go into the promised land. We know that we have done wrong."

But they were not sorry for their sins. They were only afraid of the punishment God had given them.

Moses warned, "It is too late for you to change your minds now. God will not be with you."

They would not listen to him. They climbed to the top of the hill, where the Amalekites and the Canaanites lived. As soon as these people saw all the Israelites swarming up their hill, they came out in a hurry. They shot at them with their bows and arrows, chasing them down the hill again, just as angry bees chase an enemy. The Israelites could not fight against them, for God would not help them.

The Israelites finally saw that there was no use in their trying to go into the land of Canaan, since God would not go with them. So they turned about and went back into the wild desert.

They hated to go back. They were in a very ugly frame of mind. They blamed Moses and Aaron for all their troubles, instead of blaming themselves. Some of them even rebelled against Moses, not wanting him for a leader.

One man named Korah, and another man named Dathan, and a third named Abiram, got together and decided not to obey Moses any longer. They believed themselves to be just as good as Moses.

Gathering two hundred and fifty men, they started a rebellion against Moses and Aaron. They all went to Moses and Aaron, and accused Moses and Aaron of taking too much authority. Moses and Aaron, they said, were no better than anyone else.

Korah and his men had forgotten how Moses had saved their lives. Twice God had been on the point of killing the rebellious Israelites to start a new nation with Moses, but Moses had pleaded so meekly with God to have mercy upon them that God had listened to him.

Moses did not speak angrily to them now. The next day, he answered them, God would tell which He had chosen. And then he repeated what they had said to him, "You take too much upon you, you sons of Levi." God had made them Levites, and now these wicked men wanted the priesthood, too.

A little later, Moses sent to call Korah, Dathan, and Abiram to come to him. But they were feeling very rebellious toward Moses because they had had to turn back into the wilderness.

They challenged, "We will not come. You have taken us out of the pleasant land of Egypt just to kill us in this wilderness. You want to make yourself a king over us. That is the only reason why you brought us here into this wilderness.

"You promised to bring us into a land flowing with milk and honey, and to give us fields and vineyards, and you have not done it.

"We will not come. We will not obey you any more."

Moses was indignant. He went to God to seek comfort. He said to God, "Do not accept their offering. I have not taken one ass away from them. I have not hurt a single one of them."

Then Moses said to Korah, "Tomorrow let each one of your two hundred fifty men take a censer and put coals of fire in it, and put incense on the coals. Aaron also will take a censer with fire and incense. God will choose between you and Aaron."

Part 2 — Korah's Punishment

The next day, when Korah and his company of two hundred fifty men came with their censers to the door of the Tabernacle, Moses told all the people of Israel to come too. No doubt, there were a great many others among the Israelites who also were rebellious in their hearts, and who sympathized with Korah.

Suddenly the glory of the Lord, that brilliant dazzling light, appeared to all the congregation. The Lord spoke to Moses and Aaron, "Separate yourselves from among this congregation, that I may consume them in a moment."

Moses and Aaron fell on their faces before the Lord, and prayed for the people. Would the Lord be angry with *all* the people, because of one man's sin?

God answered that all the people must get away from the tents of Korah, Dathan, and Abiram.

When all the people had moved back, Dathan, and Abiram were left standing in the doors of their tents, with their wives and their little children. And Korah stood there.

Moses spoke to all the people, and said that if these men should die like other men, then the Lord had not sent him. But if the Lord should do something new, if the earth should open her mouth and swallow them up, then the Israelites might know that these men had done wrong, and that God had punished them immediately.

Just at that moment the earth under them opened with a great crack. Korah and all the others — screaming men, women, and children — went down into the crack, with their tents and everything that they had. The earth closed over them again, and they were gone.

The terror-stricken people rushed away from that awful spot, for they were afraid that the earth would open and swallow them up, too.

In another moment a stream of fire came down from heaven and burned up all the rest of the two hundred fifty men who had been with Korah.

You no doubt will wonder why God killed the wives and the little children of Dathan and Abiram. You may be sure that God did not kill a single one that was not sinful in his heart. God is the judge of all the earth, and He always does right.

Undoubtedly these men had shown for a long time, in their talk at home, how much they hated Moses. And undoubtedly the wives had talked, too. Perhaps they were the first to suggest that they should rebel against Moses. And the children had heard the talk, and very likely they, too, hated Moses deep down in their hearts. Besides, God sometimes punishes children and grandchildren for the sins of their fathers. But Korah's sons did not die.

Hating Moses was not the worst part of their sin. It was not Moses who was leading Israel. It was God. Moses was only a servant of God.

How could any Israelite, after he had seen God's wonderful works — in making Pharaoh let the people go, in making the Red Sea go back, in speaking right out of heaven to the children of Israel on Mount Sinai, in giving them manna — how could any Israelite help knowing that it was God who was leading the people?

It is very plain that Korah and his company had not learned it. After all that God had done, they had not learned to fear Him, to love Him, and to obey Him.

And I am afraid that there were a great many others in the congregation of Israel who were not truly religious and who did not really worship God.

For the very next day, all the children of Israel began to find fault with Moses and Aaron, saying, "You have killed the people of the Lord."

How dared they speak so? It shows plainly that many of them did not truly worship God in their hearts, or they would have realized that it was God and not Moses, who had killed these rebellious men.

But while the people were speaking against Moses and Aaron, the glory of the Lord again appeared over the Tabernacle. The Lord commanded Moses and Aaron to leave the disobedient people, so that He might destroy them in a moment.

And again Moses and Aaron fell down on their faces to beg the Lord not to destroy all the Israelites.

Moses said to Aaron, "Quickly take a censer, and put in it holy fire from the altar, and put incense upon the fire. Go quickly to the

Moses looked long at the beautiful country spread out before his eyes.

Deuteronomy 34

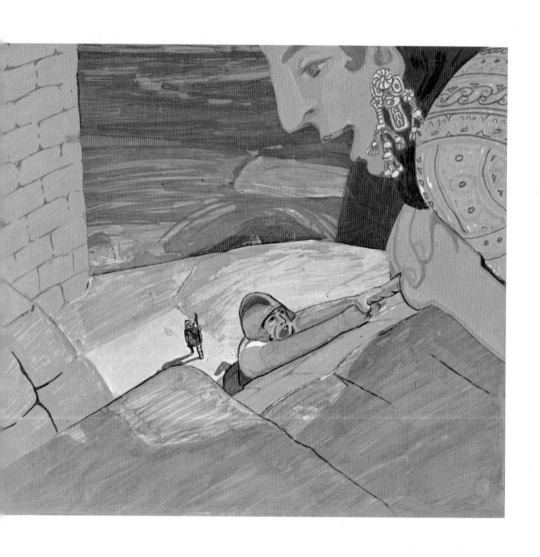

Rahab let the men down out of her window. Joshua 2

people and make atonement for them, for the Lord's anger is shown. God has sent the plague among them to punish them; they are already dying. Hurry!"

Aaron hurried to get the censer ready. He ran quickly among the people to make an atonement. He stood between the living and the dead and the plague was stopped.

In that short time, fourteen thousand seven hundred people died of the plague.

God is just. There was not one of that fourteen thousand dead who was not guilty in his heart. God took away from the Israelites the ones whose hearts were not right before God, and so cleansed His people. Those who were left were those who loved God truly and who worshipped Him with their whole hearts.

CHAPTER 50

Some Strange Happenings in the Desert
Part 1 — Two Miracles

NUMBERS 17, 20, 21, 34

The children of Israel had grumbled so much against Moses and Aaron, that God said He would show them plainly by a sign that He wanted Aaron to be priest, and not one of them.

God told Moses to tell the children of Israel that the prince of each tribe should bring to Moses a rod or stick with his name written upon it. Since Aaron was the prince of the tribe of Levi, his name must be written upon the rod of the tribe of Levi.

Moses was to put all these rods in the innermost room of the Tabernacle, in front of the golden Ark.

The next day Moses went back into the Holy of Holies and brought out the rods, giving them back to the princes.

Eleven of the rods were nothing but dry sticks, just as they had been before. But Aaron's rod was full of beautiful pink almond blossoms. There even were clusters of ripe almond nuts hanging on it!

In this way God showed the Israelites that it was Aaron whom He had chosen as priest. God told Moses to take Aaron's rod that budded and put it into the holy Ark, along with the pot of manna, and the tables with the Ten Commandments written upon them. This would keep the rebels from any further murmuring against Aaron.

Aaron and his sons were to be God's priests forever, and all the men of the tribe of Levi were to help with the work about the Tabernacle.

None of the common people might come into the Tabernacle inside the beautiful curtains. The Levites might come there to remove the ashes, to wash the silver platters, and to bring wood for the Altar.

Only the priests, Aaron and his two sons, were allowed to light the golden Candlestick, and to burn incense on the Altar of incense, and to put show-bread on the golden Table, and to offer sacrifices on the big brass Altar. No one but the high priest was ever to come into the Holy of Holies behind the Veil. If any one should, he would die.

The priests and the Levites would not be given any land in Canaan. Their part was to be priests of God. He was their inheritance. But although the priests were not to have any land, God provided for their wants by giving to them the offerings of the Israelites, the best of the oil and wine and wheat. God taught the Israelites that they must support their priests, just as we now pay a salary to our ministers.

After the Israelites were turned back into the desert, they wandered about until they came again to the desert of Zin. Here Miriam, the sister of Moses, died and was buried.

In this dry desert there was no water for the people to drink, and they again grumbled against Moses and Aaron, blaming them for all their troubles.

Why had Moses brought them out of Egypt into this evil place? There were no figs here, nor pomegranates, nor grapes. There was not even any water to drink.

Moses and Aaron went to the door of the Tabernacle and fell on their faces. They saw the glory of the Lord and heard His voice telling Moses to gather the children of Israel in front of the great rock. Moses must take his rod and speak to the rock, and plenty of water would come out of it.

So Moses gathered all the people together in front of the big rock.

Moses was very angry with the people. They were forever grumbling. They did not thank him when he had begged the Lord over and over again not to kill them all. In the end, they had even rebelled against him and had tried to set up another leader. No wonder Moses' anger was aroused. Yet he ought to have been patient with them still.

But now Moses was so angry that he lost his temper. Instead of speaking to the rock as God had told him to do, Moses lifted up his stick and struck the rock twice. In an angry tone he said, "Hear now, you rebels, must we bring you water out of this rock?"

A great stream of water burst out of the rock, enough for all the people and all their cattle. But God was not pleased with Moses for striking the rock instead of speaking to it as God had commanded.

God punished Moses and Aaron for not believing Him; neither one of them would come into the land of Canaan, but both would die in the desert. This was a terrible disappointment to Moses. After leading the people all those years through the dreary desert, he himself would not be allowed to come into the land of promise.

PART 2 — THE DEATH OF AARON

The children of Israel were now wandering in the desert of Zin, which you found on your maps once before as you followed the journey. The people wandered over the land from one place to another, as far as the Red Sea, and back again to the Mountains of Seir.

How tired and discouraged they became! How often they wished that they had trusted God when the spies brought their reports of the giants living in the land of Canaan! God had conquered all their enemies, and they should have believed that He would help to overcome the giants.

But it was useless now for them to wish they had trusted God. They must go on wandering in this hot desert until they died. Not one of them would ever see the beautiful land of promise.

How did they get new clothes when they needed them in that lonesome desert? Where could they buy new shoes when their old ones wore out?

For all their bad behavior toward God, He took wonderful care of them. In all those forty years of wandering, He provided for their clothes and their shoes so that they never lacked. Every day God sent them fresh manna to eat. They could eat it raw, or fry it, or boil it, or make cakes of it and bake it. It was delicious any way they ate it.

After a while the older people died one after the other, and the children grew up. God was leading them nearer and nearer to the land of Canaan. They had been in the desert for almost forty years, and soon God would lead them into the promised land.

But this time they were not going to take the nearest way — by the south. They were to go around to the eastern side. They had been near Mount Seir for a long time. God told Moses that the children of Israel must now turn northward.

Obeying God, Israel now came to the land of Edom. You remember that Mount Seir was the country where Esau went to live after he had parted from his brother Jacob.

That was more than four hundred years earlier, but Esau's descendants still lived there. They were called Edomites, and their country was called Edom.

As the Israelites came near to Edom, Moses sent messengers to the king, asking permission to go through his country and promising not to harm the land or its inhabitants.

But the king of Edom was very much afraid of this great host of Israelites. Since he did not trust them to keep their promises, he refused to let them go through his country.

God would not let the Israelites fight the Edomites, because they were children of Abraham, descended from Esau. He had given this part of the country to them.

So the Israelites did not pass through the country of Edom but made a long journey around it. They had to go around Mount Seir, and down to Ezion-gaber, which is by the Red Sea. Then they turned northward and came to the wilderness of Moab.

At last they came to Mount Hor, on the eastern border of Edom. Aaron, the high priest, was now a very old man.

God foretold to Moses that this was the place where Aaron was to die. He directed Moses to take Aaron and his son Eleazar into the high mountain. Aaron must give the high-priestly robes to his son Eleazar, for Aaron must die on Mount Hor.

All the people saw them starting off. After they had said "Good-bye," they stood and watched their priest go up to die. They knew that he would never come back again.

While they watched him, tears rolled down their cheeks. Never again would they see his dear face, and see his hands raised in blessing upon the tribes of Israel. Never again would they hear his sweet old voice saying,

"The Lord bless thee and keep thee.

"The Lord make His face to shine upon thee.

"The Lord lift up His countenance upon thee, and give thee peace."

At last they were out of sight upon the height of the mountain. Moses took off Aaron's beautiful high-priestly robes, and put them upon Eleazar, his son. Moses and Eleazar tenderly kissed Aaron. And Aaron folded his hands; his eyes closed, and his spirit went to live with God.

Now Eleazar was the high priest. The children of Israel mourned a whole month for Aaron.

Once more the people continued their journey. They were still traveling through the wilderness. Sad to say, they again grumbled against God, and against Moses: "Why have you brought us up out of Egypt? To die in this wilderness? For there is no bread here, nor any water, and we are tired of this manna."

The Lord sent poisonous serpents among the people to punish them for their grumbling. The snakes bit them, and a great many people died.

This time the people behaved better than their fathers had. They came to Moses in sorrow, saying, "We know that we have sinned, for we have spoken against the Lord and against thee. Pray to the Lord that He take away the serpents from us."

Moses prayed for the people, and the Lord told him to make a fiery serpent out of brass and put it on a pole where all the people could see it. If anyone had been bitten and looked up at the brass serpent, he would get well.

In the same way, any sinner may find salvation by lifting up his eyes and looking at Christ on the cross.

CHAPTER 51

God Gives Victory

NUMBERS 21

After the Israelites had been wandering in the desert for thirty-eight years, all the older people were dead except Moses, Caleb, and Joshua. There was not one left of those who had sinned against God by refusing to go into the Promised Land at the time when Canaan was spied out.

The young children were grown up. God was leading them gradually nearer to Canaan. They must have trusted God more than their fathers and mothers had, for at one time when they reached a place where there was no water, they did not grumble as their fathers had.

The Lord said to Moses, "Gather the people together and I will give them water."

Moses commanded them to dig a well with their walking sticks, and the Lord would fill it with water. The people made a song about this happening and often sang it.

They had now come to the land of Moab, where the Moabites and Ammonites lived. These people were the descendants of Lot, Abraham's nephew.

Here, as in many of these lands, wicked giants had once lived. God had helped the children of Lot to destroy these giants, called Zamzummims. Before Esau came to live in Mount Seir, giants had lived there also, but God had helped the children of Esau to conquer them. The children of Israel need not have been so much afraid of the giants in the land of Canaan, for the Lord would surely have helped them, as He had helped the children of Esau and the children of Lot.

God had given the land of Moab to the descendants of Lot, and so the Israelites went around, not attempting to pass through.

They crossed the River Arnon and came to the country of the Amorites. These were wicked heathen who worshipped a dreadful idol called Chemosh. God wanted these people to be destroyed, for they did only evil in the sight of God. He told the Israelites to fight the Amorites. He promised to help the Israelites to overcome them.

From this time on, the Israelites would have to do a great deal of fighting, for these nations must be destroyed for their wickedness. God would make them afraid of the Israelites, so that they would not have courage to fight. Then God would give their land to His people.

The Amorites soon heard that a great nation called the children of Israel had come up out of Egypt, and that they were near Canaan. What frightened them most was that these people had a God more powerful than any other, probably more powerful even than Chemosh.

"What shall we do?" the Amorites cried. "They will kill us all."

Moses sent messengers to Sihon, king of the Amorites, asking permission to pass through the country and promising not to trample down the fields or eat the grapes in the vineyards.

But Sihon would not let the Israelites pass through his country. He took all his soldiers and came out to fight against Israel. The Israelites were all ready for them. There were six hundred thousand strong men ready to fight. Above all, they had God for their helper.

And so the children of Israel won a glorious victory over the Amorites. There were many big cities with high walls. The Israelites destroyed all the cities, because of the wickedness of the people.

All the cattle — the sheep and cows, asses and camels and goats — the children of Israel saved. God permitted them to take all these animals for themselves. And He gave them the houses of the Amorites, with the vineyards and olive orchards, and all the other good things they found there.

At last they were out of the dreary desert and were living in a beautiful land.

But they did not stop here. On they went, still further north to the country of Bashan. This country was full of high-walled cities, ruled over by a king named Og.

Now Og was a terrible giant. He is said to have had an iron bedstead which was thirteen feet long, so he must have been twelve feet tall — about twice as tall as ordinary men.

King Og came out with all his armies to fight against the people of God. How frightened the Israelites were, when they saw that terrible giant coming out to fight them!

The Lord reassured them, "Fear him not, for I have delivered him into your hand, and all his people, and his land. And you shall do to him as you did to Sihon, king of the Amorites."

That day the Israelites won another great victory. They slew the giant and all his people. There were sixty big cities in the land of Bashan. The Israelites fought against these walled cities, overcoming every one of them. They also conquered a great many small cities which had no walls. No city was strong enough to stand against them.

God commanded them to kill all the people, for they were very wicked. All the cities and possessions of the heathen people, God gave to the Israelites.

The Israelites had now conquered all the country from the River Arnon to Mount Hermon. Find these places on your map. See what a big country Canaan once was.

CHAPTER 52

Balaam Displeases a Frightened King

NUMBERS 22, 23, 24, 25.

PART 1 — WHY THE KING WAS AFRAID

After the children of Israel had conquered the two kings of the Amorites, Sihon and Og, they settled for a time in the plains of Moab. This was a rich and grassy country with plenty of fine food for their flocks and herds. What a comfort it was to the Israelites to be in a fertile country, where they could have grapes and olives and all the fruits they liked.

In front of them was the Jordan River. Behind their camp were several mountains or high hills. One of them was called Pisgah; and another, Nebo. From the tops of these hills, one could see the tents of the Israelites spreading out in every direction like a sea.

In the land where they now were, there was a nation called the Midianites. These people did not live always in the same place. They were a wandering nation, much like gypsies. Just now they were living in Moab under their king, Balak.

King Balak had been hearing about the children of Israel for many years. Time and again reports had reached him about the wonderful God of the Israelites, so much more powerful than the god of the Midianites, Baal-peor. Balak had heard how the God of the Israelites sent dreadful plagues upon the land of Egypt, and how He brought the Israelites through the Red Sea and destroyed the Egyptian army.

Now he heard how Sihon fought against Israel, and how he and all his people had been killed. Even the terrible giant, Og, had been killed, and all his people.

And here were these Israelites right in his country! Balak was terribly frightened, and his princes were just as much afraid as he.

What should they do? It was of no use to try to fight them. Sihon and Og had done that, and they had been killed. The God of the Israelites was very powerful, and He would surely help His people.

No, they must think of some other way to drive out this great multitude of Israelites.

After Balak had thought and thought about what he should do to overcome the Israelites, an idea came to him. As I have said before, Balak and his people wandered from one place to another. They had once lived in the land of Assyria, where the mighty Euphrates River ran. Balak knew that in this country there was a prophet of the Lord, named Balaam.

Balaam was not an Israelite. We do not know how he came to be a prophet of the true God. There must have been some people in his country who still worshipped Jehovah.

Balak decided to send to the far-away country, where he had once lived, asking the prophet Balaam to come and curse the people of Israel. That would be just the thing to do for Balaam was a prophet of the same God that the Israelites served.

It was more than three hundred fifty miles away. Even though they rode on asses, the messengers would have to journey a whole week. At last they reached Pethor, where Balaam lived. They gave the prophet Balak's message. They had brought rich presents as a reward for Balaam if he would curse the Israelites.

Balaam asked them to stay all night. He said he would ask the Lord whether he could go with the men and curse Israel, as Balak wanted him to do.

In the night God spoke to Balaam and said, "You shall not go with them, and you shall not curse the people, for they are blessed."

In the morning Balaam said to the messengers, "You can go home again, for the Lord will not let me go with you."

The princes went back to King Balak, saying, "Balaam refused to come with us."

Balak was desperate. He sent other messengers, more noble than the first ones, promising to do anything Balaam should ask him, if he would only curse this people for him.

And Balaam answered, "If King Balak would give me his house full of silver and gold, I cannot do what God will not let me do."

Balaam, although he was a prophet of God, did not love God and did not want to please Him. He was afraid of God and did not dare to disobey Him. But he did want to go with the messengers and earn the rich rewards that the king had promised.

He knew that God did not want him to go and curse Israel. He ought to have told the princes to go right back home again. Instead he said, "Stay all night with me and I will see what God says to me."

At night God told Balaam that he might go with the men, but he was to say only what God would tell him. So in the morning Balaam saddled his ass and went with the men.

PART 2 — AN ANIMAL TALKS

God was angry with His prophet, for Balaam knew well enough that God did not want him to go.

God sent an angel against Balaam. The ass saw the angel standing in the way. She turned aside out of the path and went into the field. Since Balaam did not see the angel, he struck the ass to make her go back into the road.

The angel then stood some distance farther along the road, at a place where there was a wall on each side of the road. When the ass came to this place and saw the angel, she was afraid. She pushed herself just as close to the wall as she could, hurting Balaam by crushing his foot against the wall.

Balaam, who did not see the angel with the sword, was very angry to have the ass balk so. He gave his animal a hard beating with his stick, for his foot hurt.

Then the angel went still farther, and stood in a very narrow place where there was no room to turn, either to the right or to the left. When the ass came to this place and saw the angel with the drawn sword, she fell down under Balaam.

Balaam was furiously angry to have his ass behave in this way. He laid blow after blow on the back of the poor animal.

Then God opened the mouth of the ass. "What have I done to you that you have beaten me these three times?"

Balaam said, "You have disobeyed me. If I had a sword in my hand, I would kill you."

The ass answered, "Haven't I always been a good ass? Have I ever disobeyed you before?"

And Balaam said, "No."

Then the Lord opened the eyes of Balaam. He, too, saw the angel with the drawn sword in his hand. His guilty heart told him that the angel had come to punish him for disobeying God. He bowed down his head with fear and fell flat on his face.

The angel said to him, "Why have you beaten your ass these three times? I came out to oppose you, because you are going against my wishes. Your ass saw me and turned away from me these three times. If she had not done this, I would have killed you, and saved her alive."

Balaam knew he was doing wrong to go with these men, and that **though** God had given him permission to go, He did not want him to.

Balaam said very humbly to the angel, "I have sinned. I did not **know** that you were standing in the way against me. And now, if you wish me to, I will go back."

"No," said the angel. "Go with the men; but only the word that I shall give you, that you shall speak."

King Balak was waiting anxiously at home to see whether Balaam would really come to him. When he heard that Balaam was coming, he was so much pleased that he went out to meet him.

He said to Balaam. "Did I not earnestly call you the first time? Then why did you not come to me? Am I not able to promote you to great honor?"

Balaam answered, "Well, I have come now; but I have no power to say anything, except what God tells me to say."

The next day King Balak took Balaam up on a high hill, so that he could look around and see the tents of the Israelites spread out in every direction. He told his servants to build seven altars on the hill, and to bring seven bullocks and seven rams for sacrifice. Then Balaam offered a bullock and a ram on each altar.

When the sacrifices had been finished, Balaam said to King Balak, "Stand here by your offerings, and I will go a little farther off — perhaps God will come and speak to me."

Then God came to meet Balaam and told him what to say to King Balak. The prophet returned to the place where the king and all his nobles waited to hear Balaam curse the Israelites. Balaam recited what God had said to him, as if he were reciting poetry. This is a part of what he said:

"How shall I curse whom God hath not cursed?
And how shall I defy whom Jehovah hath not defied?
Who can count the dust of Jacob?
Or number the fourth part of Israel?"

King Balak and his princes were astonished. Balaam had not cursed the Israelites at all. He had blessed them. When the king reproached him, Balaam answered, "Must I not be careful to say what God said to me?"

King Balak said, "Come, and I will take you to another place, and you shall not see them all, but only a few of them."

So he took Balaam to the top of a high mountain called Pisgah. Again he had his servants build seven altars, again he offered a bullock and a ram on each altar, so that the God of the Israelites would be favorable to him.

Balaam stood at a little distance and listened to what God had to say to him. Then he went back to the altars, where King Balak and all his princes were eagerly waiting to hear.

Again Balaam disappointed Balak. He said, "Behold, I have received commandment to bless, and He hath blessed, and I cannot reverse it."

How disappointed King Balak was! He said, "Do not bless them nor curse them. Do not do anything at all."

Balaam answered, "Did I not tell you that I must say everything that God tells me to say?"

Part 3 — Balaam Works Against God

"Then come to another place, and perhaps God will let you curse them from there," said King Balak.

So they went to the top of another high mountain, called Peor, which you can find on your map. Here also King Balak made sacrifices to please the God of the Israelites.

From this high place, Balaam could see all the tents of the Israelites spread out in the plains of Moab. The spirit of God came upon him. He fell into a trance; that is, he began to speak as if he were speaking in a dream — but his eyes were open. He spoke in poetry, saying:

> "How goodly are thy tents, O Jacob,
> Thy tabernacles, O Israel! . . .
> Blessed be everyone that blesseth thee,
> And cursed be everyone that curseth thee."

Balak was furious to hear Balaam bless Israel. He said, "I called you to curse my enemies, and now you have blessed them three times. Go home as fast as you can. I was going to give you great honors, but I shall not give you anything now."

Once more Balaam answered, "Did I not tell you, King Balak, that if you were to give me your house full of silver and gold, I could not say one word, bad or good, except just what the Lord tells me to say?

"Now I am going back home, but before I go, I will tell you what will happen in the days that are to come."

Then Balaam spoke some more wonderful words which God put into his mouth. He foretold the most marvelous thing that ever came to pass — the coming of Jesus Christ, the Savior of the world. He said:

> "There shall come forth a Star out of Jacob,
> And a Scepter shall rise out of Israel."

I have told you that though Balaam knew the true God and heard His voice, he was not a good man at all. While he was prophesying for King Balak, he said only the words that God put into his mouth. He did not dare to curse the children of Israel, although he would have liked to curse them, to get the riches that the king had promised him.

He did a very wicked thing. Perhaps he did it to get some of the money that King Balak had promised. He went among the Midianites and said to them, "I will tell you how you can make their God angry with them so that He will destroy them.

"Go and visit the Israelites. Be very friendly with them — even marry some of them. Then, when you are good friends with them, invite them to some of your idol feasts. Tell them to come and worship your god, Baal-peor. Then their God will be angry with them and will kill them."

Wasn't that a wicked thing for Balaam to do? He very well knew that this heathen idol was only an image made of wood and stone; that Jehovah was the only true God. And yet he stayed with the Midianites to try to make the Israelites worship their idol.

When the Israelites began to worship the idol, Jehovah was angry, as Balaam had known. Then He sent a plague upon the Israelites to punish them for worshipping idols. It was so deadly that twenty-four thousand people died.

CHAPTER 53

The Israelites Numbered Again

NUMBERS 26, 31, 32

The people were encamped now in the land of Moab. Just on the other side of the Jordan was the city of Jericho. The forty years were nearly over, and they were waiting till God should tell them to cross the river and march into the promised land.

Something else had to be done first, however. Moses and Eleazer — he who was now the high priest — were to number the children of Israel. All the men who were twenty years or older were to be counted.

It was necessary to find out the number of strong men who could fight. Soon they would cross over into the land of Canaan, where they would have to fight many battles with the fierce heathen who lived there.

You remember that the children of Israel were numbered forty years earlier when they first came out of Egypt. Since then, the men numbered in the earlier counting had died, and their children had taken their places.

There was another reason for taking the census. After the Israelites had taken possession of Canaan, a piece of land was to be given to every man except the Levites, who were to serve in the Tabernacle.

I am sure you will want to know how many Israelites there were. In eleven of the tribes there were six hundred one thousand, seven hundred thirty strong men, able to fight. The Levites were counted separately, twenty-three thousand of them.

Counting all the people — men, women, and children — Moses and Eleazar found that there were more than three million Israelites. There was not one left who had been counted in the first numbering forty years before, except Caleb and Joshua. All the others had died.

After Moses and Eleazar finished this task, God told Moses that the Israelites must go to war against the Midianites, to punish that nation for inviting the Israelites to their idol feasts and teaching them to bow down to their god.

Each of the twelve tribes had to send a thousand armed men to the war. Phineas, Eleazar's son, went along — not to fight, for he was a priest, but to blow the trumpets.

So the Israelites fought with the Midianites, killing all the men and their five kings. They killed the wicked Balaam, too. They burned all the cities and all the castles.

The soldiers brought with them a great many thousand cattle and sheep, for the country was green and fertile, and the Midianites had great flocks and herds. They took a great deal of silver, gold, iron, tin, and lead.

Moses made the soldiers give half of these things to the rest of the people, who had not gone out to the battle. Other things he made them give to the Levites.

After the battle, the captains counted all the soldiers. They found that not one of the Israelites had been killed. They were so thankful to God for taking such fine care of them that they brought to the Tabernacle as a present to the Lord the golden jewelry which they had taken from the Midianites.

Three of the tribes — Reuben, Gad, and half of Manasseh — liked the plains of Moab so well that they asked Moses if they could stay there, instead of crossing the Jordan with the rest of the tribes.

The land of Moab was rich and fertile, and the grass grew green and long. It was just the place for cows and sheep. The tribes of Reuben, Gad, and the half tribe of Manasseh had very large flocks of cows and sheep.

Moses said that they might keep Moab, if they would promise to go over the Jordan with the rest of the Israelites to help them fight against the heathen in the land of Canaan. They said they would help, if Moses would first let them build houses and cities for their wives and children, and folds for their sheep.

So Moses gave the fertile plains of Moab to the tribe of Reuben; and the kingdom of Sihon, king of the Amorites, to the tribe of Gad; and the kingdom of Og to the half tribe of Manasseh.

Once more God spoke to Moses. He told him to tell the children of Israel, "When you pass over the River Jordan into the land of Canaan, you must drive out the heathen who live there; you must destroy all their pictures of their heathen idols, and all their gold and silver images, and break down all their altars."

God knew that if they should leave any idols or any altars, in the course of time they would worship idols. If God had let the heathen people live, the Israelites would have become heathen, too.

After they had conquered Canaan, the princes must divide the land and give every man a piece of land for a farm, except the Levites. The Levites should live in cities. Around each city must be enough ground for their cows and sheep, but no farm-lands. They should have forty-eight cities. Six of these cities should be cities of refuge — three on each side of the Jordan.

If anyone should kill another person without meaning to do so, he might run into one of these cities of refuge. In that city he would be safe from punishment.

CHAPTER 54

The Last Words of Moses

NUMBERS 27; DEUTERONOMY 3, 31, 34

Moses had been the leader of the children of Israel for forty years. Now he was old, and his work on earth was nearly done.

God had told Moses that he could not go over the Jordan into the beautiful land they were about to enter, because he did not honor God when he struck the rock to bring water out of it.

Moses begged God to let him go into the promised land with the children of Israel, but God would not. Instead, God told Moses that He would show him the beautiful land from the top of a high mountain.

Moses wondered what would become of the children of Israel when he was not there to lead them. He asked God to appoint another man in his place. Moses loved the people of Israel, because they were God's people.

So God chose Joshua. And Moses brought Joshua to the priest Eleazar, before all the people. For the priest would pray to God for Joshua. There Moses laid his hands on Joshua's head and told him that he must lead the people into the promised land.

Before Moses left, he called all the people together to remind them of many things they must not forget. The people listened, for they knew that in a few days their old leader would be gone from them forever and they would no longer hear his voice.

Moses reminded them that no other nation had ever been so close to God. They must not forget all the things God had done for them, and they must surely tell their children about Him. He warned them again to destroy the heathen nations of the land, because God had chosen the Israelites as His holy people. If they would obey Him; the Lord would bless them richly; if they would not keep His commandments, He would surely punish them.

Moses wrote down all the laws of God and gave the rolls to the priests to keep. He commanded them to call a great meeting, of men, women and children and even strangers, once in seven years, and to read this law to them. Besides that, he told mothers and fathers to tell their children about God and His law every day.

Moses wrote the first five books of the Bible. He did not write them by himself, but God told him exactly what to write, for these books were to teach Israel and all the world about the Lord.

These books must be carefully kept. So Moses gave them to the Levites and commanded that they should be put beside the sacred Ark of the Covenant in the inner room of the Tabernacle, the Holy of Holies. This was the very safest place for them.

Moses had two great works to do in his life. One was to bring the children of Israel out of the land of Egypt into Canaan. It was a very great task to lead three million people and great herds of cattle for forty years, through terrible desert land. Moses could never have done it alone, but God helped him. When God has a great work for any man to do, He always helps him.

The other great work Moses had to do was the writing of the first five books of the Bible. This task was very important, because these books are God's Word to man.

But now his work was finished. And although Moses was a hundred and twenty years old, he was as strong and well as a young man. His eyes were still clear and bright, and he could walk with a quick step. God had given Moses good health.

When the day came that he must die, God told Moses to write a song and teach it to the people. Singing it would help them remember about God. Moses and Joshua taught the song to the people. That was the very last thing Moses had to do.

God said to Joshua, "Be strong and of a good courage, for you shall bring the children of Israel into the land which I promised them, and I shall be with you."

After God had given Joshua this charge, Moses bade the people a last goodbye and gave them his blessing. You may be sure that there were tears in the eyes of many of the people.

Moses raised his hands and gave a beautiful blessing to each of the twelve tribes. At the end he said:

> "The eternal God is thy dwelling place,
> And underneath are the everlasting arms . . .
> Happy art thou, O Israel.
> Who is like unto thee,
> A people saved by Jehovah!"

Then he went up Mount Nebo. From the top of the mount he looked around. He saw the beautiful valley of Jericho, and off to the west the great Mediterranean Sea. The air was clear, and God showed him the land far away in every direction. He looked long at the beautiful country spread out before his eyes. He was happy to know that this land was where his beloved people would soon be living in peace. And his heart was filled with love to God for His goodness.

Then Moses lay down, and his spirit went to live with God. God Himself buried Moses in a valley in the land of Moab, in a place no man knew.

There has never been another man in all the world who spent two whole months in God's presence, to talk with the Lord face to face.

For thirty days the children of Israel wept for Moses.

And Joshua was full of the spirit of wisdom, for Moses had laid his hands on him. The children of Israel now looked for him to lead them.

CHAPTER 55

Canaan At Last

JOSHUA 1-5

PART 1 — RAHAB AND THE SPIES

After the death of Moses, God spoke to Joshua and told him to lead the people into the land of Canaan, for God had given the whole land to them. God promised to be with Joshua, as He had been with Moses, if he would obey God's law.

Having been instructed by Joshua, the officers told the people to cook a lot of food to take with them. In three days they were going into the land of Canaan. Everyone was delighted. At last! At last! In three days they were to enter the promised land!

All the housewives began to cook and bake. They still ate the daily manna from heaven, but now they could eat many other things, too. Did not the flocks and herds of the Midianites belong to them?

Just across the Jordan River was the big city of Jericho, with high stone walls around it, and big iron gates which were shut every night, so that no enemies could come in. This was the first town that the Israelites would have to conquer. So Joshua sent two spies to Jericho, to find out the easiest way to get into the city.

The spies managed to get into the city secretly. They went to the house of a woman named Rahab, with whom they stayed.

For a long time, Rahab, as well as the other Canaanites, had been hearing wonderful stories of the power and might of the God of the Israelites. She did not wish to try to fight against this great God and His people, as the other Canaanites did. Although she had been a heathen all her life, there came into her heart the thought that it would be better to take this great God for her own and to try to help His people.

When the two spies came into her house, she took them upstairs to the flat roof of her house, and told them to lie down. Then she covered them over with stalks of flax, which was like hay, so that they could not be seen.

A few persons happened to see the two spies come into Jericho and go into Rahab's house. They ran to the king and said in their excitement, "O king, do you known that there are two men of the Israelites who came into our city today? They are spies, surely."

The king sent in great haste to Rahab, ordering her to bring out those men who had come into her house.

She said, "Two men did come in here, but I did not know who they were. When it was dark, just before the gates of the city were shut, the men went out again. I do not know where they went, but if you go after them, you may overtake them."

Rahab was a heathen, and probably did not know that it is wrong to tell lies.

The messengers left her house, hurrying after the spies. As soon as they had gone out of the gates, the keepers shut the gates, so that no other spies could come in.

Rahab hurried up to the men on the roof, and she said to them, "I know that the Lord has given you the land. Everyone here is in terror of you. We have heard how the Lord dried up the water of the Red Sea for you when you came out of Egypt, and what you did to the two kings of the Amorites on the other side of the Jordan, Sihon and Og, whom you destroyed. When we heard these things, our hearts melted with fear. Not one of us had any courage left.

"Now promise me that since I have been kind to you, you will also show me kindness, and save my father and mother and brothers and sisters, and all that they have, when you comt into Jericho with your armies.

The two spies promised not to kill her nor any of her family, if she would promise not to tell anyone what they had come for.

Now the city wall was so thick that houses were built on the top of it, or in it. Rahab lived in one of these houses. Some of her windows were over the wall, looking out into the country.

Rahab said to the men, "The gates are shut now, so you can't get out that way. I will let you down out of my window into the open country with this scarlet rope. You can go to the mountains and hide yourselves for three days, till the men who are hunting for you have come back. Then it will be safe for you to go home."

The men in turn said, "When we come here to conquer Jericho, you must fasten this bright red rope in your window where we can see it plainly. Bring your father and mother and sisters and brothers into your own house. We promise to save all your family alive. But you must not speak a word to anyone about all this."

So Rahab let the men down out of her window into the fields outside the town. They hid in the mountains for three days.

Afterwards they went back to Joshua. They announced, "Truly the Lord has delivered all the land into our hands, for all the people faint with fear because of us."

Part 2 — The River Becomes Dry

As Joshua had commanded, the people had made everything ready. They had cooked and baked enough food to last for several days. Everything was packed and ready to be taken, except the tents in which they were going to sleep the last night.

Joshua told them to break up the camp in the plains of Moab, where they had been encamped for several months after the fight with the Midianites, and to move near the River Jordan, so that early in the morning they would be all ready to cross over the river.

After the people had heard Joshua give these directions, they went back to their tents and got ready for bed, so that they could get up as soon as it was light. What a happy people they were that night! Tomorrow they were truly going into the promised land!

Early in the morning the long procession formed. You remember that they always marched in regular order. This time, the priests went first, with God's Ark.

Now the Jordan River is wild and turbulent. At this time of year it overflowed all its banks. But just as soon as the feet of the priests stepped into the water of the river, the waters stopped flowing down. They formed a high wall, about ten miles farther up the river. The water that had already flowed down, drained away, and soon there was no more water in the river bed. The hot sun quickly dried up the mud, so that the children of Israel could walk across.

The priests with the Ark stood in the middle of the river-bed. They did not move while the long, long procession of the Israelites passed by them to the other side.

Joshua had picked out twelve strong men beforehand, and had told them that each one should pick up a big stone, as heavy as he could carry, from the bed in the middle of the river, where the priests' feet had stood; and that he should carry it to the other side. These stones must be heaped on the bank of the river.

Joshua did this so that in future times, when their children should see these twelve big stones on the bank of the river and ask, "Father, why are these stones here?" the father could answer, "My son, these stones are here to mark the very spot where God dried up the waters of the river until we all passed over the Jordan."

When all the people had passed over, Joshua commanded the priests to come up out of the river-bed. Just as soon as they stepped up on the bank on the other side of the river, the high wall of water gave way, and the waters came roaring and tumbling down and filled the river-bed again.

The children of Israel were at last, after all their wanderings, at home in the land of Canaan, which had been promised to their fathers, Abraham, Isaac, and Jacob.

They pitched their tents that night for the first time in their own country. Here they rested for a few days, because it was the time of year for their Passover to be held. They did not move until they had finished celebrating the Passover.

The day after this feast, the manna that they had been eating for forty years stopped coming. They did not need it any longer, for there was plenty of food to be had in their own country.

The Amorites and the Canaanites lived here. They were cruel heathen people, so wicked that God did not want them to live. They worshipped a brass idol called Moloch, which had the body of a man, sitting, and the head of a calf. The people worshipped this idol by building a hot fire inside it till the idol became red-hot. They put their babies and little children into the arms of this image. While the poor little child was burning to death, they beat drums, so that they could not hear its cries of anguish. In many other ways the people had been wicked for years and years. Now their time had come. God used Israel to punish them.

The people of the land had heard about the coming of the children of Israel and they were terrified; they had heard that the Israelites had a mighty God who helped them in miraculous ways. Now when they heard that the God of the Israelites had dried up the waters of the Jordan River, they were overcome with fear. What could they do against such a God as this?

CHAPTER 56

A Victory and a Defeat

Joshua 6, 7

Part 1 — Marching Around Jericho

The camp of the Israelites was very near to the city of Jericho. When the people of the city saw the Israelites coming upon them, they kept the city gates shut and locked, both day and night. No one was allowed to go out or come in.

If God had not helped the Israelites, they could never have entered the city. But the Lord told Joshua how the people might take the city.

Joshua arranged everything as God had commanded.

The women and the children stayed in their camp at Gilgal. Only the men went to fight against Jericho. First came thousands of soldiers marching in regular order. Then came seven priests with seven trumpets. Four more priests followed, bearing God's Ark on their shoulders. Last of all came other thousands of soldiers.

This procession marched around the city of Jericho. The priests blew with their trumpets as they went, but the soldiers were perfectly quiet. They did not open their mouths to speak a single word.

It took a long time to march all around the big city. When they had done it once, the soldiers went home to their tents for that day.

The people of Jericho who had houses on the wall had their windows all barred and barricaded because they were afraid that the Israelites might shoot some arrows through them. But wherever there was a little chink or crack, they peeped down to see what the Israelites were doing.

They saw the soldiers marching around the city, as still as mice, and the seven priests blowing horns. Then they saw them go home to their camp.

The next day, upon hearing the trumpets again, they looked through their peep-holes. They saw the Israelite soldiers marching around the city. Again they saw them go home to their camp without attacking the city.

For six days this happened. The first time the people of Jericho heard the trumpets and saw the soldiers marching round they were terribly frightened. "What are they going to do to us?" they asked.

But after it had happened for six days, they were no longer frightened. They boasted, "Well, if they aren't going to do anything but march around the city, it won't hurt us very much."

On the morning of the seventh day, the soldiers started very early. They were going to march around seven times, instead of only once. Six times they marched around that big city in perfect silence, except for the blowing of the horns. But the seventh time, all at once, the priests blew a loud long blast on their horns, and Joshua turned around and threw up his arms and cried, "Shout! The Lord has given you the city!"

In an instant every man threw up his arms and shouted as loud as he could. Just at that moment the walls fell down with a terrible crash. Jericho was open to all the soldiers!

The people were so surprised that they could do nothing to save themselves. The soldiers turned and ran right into the city. With their swords and spears they killed all the people of Jericho — even all the oxen, sheep, and asses. God had commanded them to destroy everything.

Only Rahab and her family and all that she had were saved. After that, Rahab lived among the Israelites and worshipped the true God for the rest of her life.

Although God had commanded the soldiers not to take any of the things they found in the city, one man, whose name was Achan, saw a very beautiful garment and a pile of silver and a big piece of gold which he wanted very much. He took them secretly to his tent. There he dug a hole in the earthen floor of the tent and hid them. He thought no one knew about it.

The soldiers saved all the silver and gold, and also the kettles of brass and iron that they found, for such things were great treasures at that time. They brought all these things into the Lord's treasury in the Tabernacle.

They burned the city. The people of Jericho were so wicked that God did not want even their houses saved. I suppose that the houses were full of heathen idols and wicked pictures. God did not want the children of Israel to live in such houses.

Jericho might never be built up again. Joshua cursed the man who should build the city again, saying that his oldest son would die at the laying of the foundations, and his youngest son would die at the completion of the work.

You would think that after a prophecy like this one, no man would every try to build up Jericho again. No one did for a long time. After five hundred years, a man who did not care anything about God thought Jericho would be a fine place to build a city, because the land was very rich and fertile there.

He started to build a city there. As soon as he had laid the foundation, his oldest son died. For all that, he went on building, but when he had finished the city and set up the gates, his youngest son died. So the curse which Joshua pronounced was fulfilled.

After the capture of Jericho, the people saw that God was with Joshua, as He had been with Moses. Joshua's fame was spread throughout the country.

PART 2 — THE DEFEAT AT AI

Near Jericho was a small town called Ai. Joshua sent some men to Ai to find out about the town.

The men came back and said to Joshua, "Ai is just a small place. We can easily conquer it. It is not necessary to send a large number of soldiers there. Two or three thousand will be enough."

Having had such a glorious victory at Jericho, the Israelites thought it would be no trouble at all to overcome Ai. But things turned out differently. The men of Ai beat the Israelites, and killed thirty-six of them. The Israelite soldiers lost all their courage, and they ran before the men of Ai.

When the people of Israel heard how their soldiers had been beaten by the men of Ai, they were much frightened.

Joshua was discouraged. He tore his clothes and put dust on his head, and the elders of Israel did the same. They fell on their faces before the Ark of the Lord. They lay there all day, weeping and praying.

Joshua said, "Would that we had been content and dwelt beyond the Jordan! Oh, Lord God, what shall I say, now that the Israelites have turned their backs before their enemies?

"For all the heathen people will hear that Israel has been beaten like this, and they will not be afraid of us any longer. They all will come and gather round us, and they will fight us and kill us all.

"O God, if we are going to be conquered, what will the heathen think about our God? They will think that our God is not powerful at all."

Joshua had lost all courage. It seemed to him that God was not keeping His promise to help him, as He had helped Moses and had promised to help him.

God heard Joshua's moaning and crying. God did not speak gently to him. He told Joshua to get up. There was a good reason why Israel had been beaten. They had sinned. They had taken some of the things out of Jericho that God commanded them not to touch. They had stolen some of these things and lied about it.

That was the reason they had been beaten by the men of Ai. God would not help them to fight any longer, until they took away the accursed things from among them.

You see, Achan had *stolen* silver and gold, for all the silver and gold belonged to the treasury of the Lord. None of the people had any right to it. He had lied, too, for he had hidden the beautiful garment and the silver and gold in the earth under his tent. He was trying to deceive Joshua and the people; and trying to deceive is lying, even if we do not speak a word that is not true.

God can see what is in our hearts, even if we have not spoken aloud, and He knew Achan was lying. The Lord commanded that all the people should come before Him in the morning, and He would tell them who was the guilty man.

Early in the morning the priests sounded the trumpets. The tribes of Israel came up, one after another. After the tribe of Judah had come up, God told Joshua that the wicked man belonged to this tribe.

Then all the families of the tribe of Judah came up, one after another, and the family of the Zarhites was taken. All the households of the Zarhites came up, man by man, and Zabdi was taken. In his family, Achan, the grandson of Zabdi, was taken.

So Joshua and all the people knew that Achan was the guilty man. Joshua said to him, "My son, tell God that you have done wrong. Tell me what you have taken. Do not tell a lie."

Achan said, "I have sinned against the Lord God of Israel. In Jericho I saw a beautiful Babylonish garment and a lot of silver and a big piece of gold, and I took them. They are hidden in the earth under my tent."

Joshua sent a man to Achan's tent. There lay the garment and the gold and silver.

Joshua said to Achan, "Why have you made all this trouble in Israel? God will trouble you this day."

All Israel took Achan, his sons and his daughters, his oxen, his asses, his sheep, his tents, and all that he had, with the garment, the silver, and the gold, and they brought them into a nearby valley. The people of Israel stoned Achan and his family with stones. After they were dead, the Israelites burned everything and threw stones over the place where the ashes were, till there was a great heap of stones on the place.

Did Achan go to Heaven? No one but God can answer that question. But I think that perhaps he did. For Achan confessed his sin, and if we confess our sins and are sorry for them, "God is faithful and just to forgive us our sins."

CHAPTER 57

How Trickery Overthrew Ai and Saved Gibeon
Joshua 8-11

Part 1 — Two Tricks

After this, God told Joshua not to be afraid or discouraged, but to take the soldiers and go up to Ai, for God would help them to conquer it. They would do to Ai and its king as they had done to Jericho and its king. This time they might have for themselves whatever they should find in the city.

Choosing thirty thousand brave soldiers, Joshua sent them to Ai at night, so that no one would see them. He commanded them to go to the other side of the town and hide themselves.

Another five thousand hid themselves on the west side of the city.

At daylight Joshua took all the rest of the soldiers and marched openly to the front of the city. The king of Ai saw the soldiers marching up to his town, but he did not know about the thirty thousand soldiers who were hiding behind the town, nor about the five thousand who were hidden on the west side. He called every single man to come out of the town to fight the Israelites. There was not one man left in the city.

Joshua and all his army pretended to be afraid. They fled, while the men of Ai ran after them.

"Stretch out your spear toward the city," commanded the Lord.

The men in hiding were watching for that signal. As soon as they saw Joshua stretch out his spear, they rose up from their hiding places and rushed toward the city. They had no trouble in entering it, for the men of Ai had left the gates wide open.

The soldiers set fire to the city. When the men of Ai looked behind them, they saw the smoke of their city rising up to the sky. Joshua

The priests blew a loud blast on their horns. Joshua 6

Each man had a trumpet, a lighted torch, and an empty pitcher to hide in.
Joshua 7

knew that his thirty thousand brave soldiers had succeeded in getting into the city. He and his men no longer pretended to be afraid of the men of Ai. They turned around and began to fight.

The other Israelite soldiers came out of the burning city and began to attack the men of Ai from that direction. The Israelites surrounded the enemy on every side. Not one escaped.

Not far away from Ai was a large city called Gibeon, one of the royal cities. The people of Gibeon were just as much afraid of the Israelites as the people of Jericho had been.

The elders of the city talked the matter over. What should they do about these Israelites? They had conquered Jericho and killed all its people; they had conquered Ai. Undoubtedly they would soon come to Gibeon. Their God, as everyone knew, had commanded their leader to destroy all the people of the land.

The Gibeonites knew that they must do something and do it quickly, or they would all be dead men. While they were talking, someone thought of a plan by which they might trick the Israelites.

All the men put on very old, dirty, ragged clothes. They wore old shoes, and they put patched wine-skins on their asses. They filled their torn bags with dried, mouldy bread.

Dressed like this, they went to see Joshua at the camp of Gilgal. They pretended to be travelers from a very far country, wanting to be friends with the Israelites.

"But you may live near here," the Israelites said. "Then how can we be friends with you?"

They answered, "We came from a far country. We have heard about your wonderful God. We have heard all the things He did in Egypt, and what He did to King Sihon and King Og. We would like to be friends with a people who have so wonderful a God.

"So we have come to make friends with you. When we started, we took this bread hot out of our houses; see how dry and mouldy it is now! These wine-bottles, which we filled when we left, were new then; see how old and torn they are! Our clothes and our shoes are old and worn out, because we have come such a long way.

"Now make peace with us, and be our friends."

Joshua and the princes of Israel made peace with them, and swore an oath by the Lord God of Israel to let them live. But they forgot one very important thing — they forgot to ask God what they should do.

After three days the children of Israel heard that the Gibeonites were not travelers and strangers at all, but that they lived very near in a large city. The Israelites were angry with their princes, because they had made peace with the Gibeonites. They wanted to make war on the city.

But the princes said, "We must let them live, because we swore an oath by the Lord God of Israel."

Joshua told the people of Gibeon that they would not be killed. Because they had so deceived the Israelites, however, they would have to become servants, to cut wood and draw water. Although the Gibeonites did not like this, they preferred slavery to death.

PART 2 — WHEN NIGHT WAS LATE

After the Gibeonites had made peace with Israel in this deceitful way, the kings of the other cities heard what they had done. They were very angry with the Gibeonites for making peace with their common enemy, the Israelites.

Adoni-zedek, the king of Jerusalem, sent word to four other kings to come and help him to fight the Gibeonites because they had gone over to the enemy. But when the Gibeonites found that the five kings were going to fight them, they sent word to Joshua, asking him to help them.

The Lord told Joshua not to be afraid of the five kings, for He would deliver them into the hands of the Israelites.

So Joshua took all his brave soldiers and marched by night upon the kings and their armies. In the morning there was a great battle. The enemies of Israel fled, and the soldiers of Israel pursued them. The Lord helped Joshua by sending a hail-storm upon the enemy.

After a while Joshua looked at the sun and saw that it was going down. But the battle was not yet ended. Then Joshua spoke to the sun and said:

> "Sun, stand thou still upon Gibeon,
> And thou, Moon, in the valley of Ajalon."

And for the only time in the history of the world, the sun stayed in its place. God granted Joshua's prayer and made the day longer for him.

When the five kings saw that their soldiers could not stand against the soldiers of Israel, they ran away and hid in a cave. Joshua heard about this and said, "Roll big stones before the opening of the cave and set soldiers to guard it. The rest of you go on pursuing the enemy, for the Lord is giving us the victory over them."

The Israelite soldiers ran on, and that day they conquered all the armies of the five kings. Afterwards they took the five kings out of the cave and hanged them.

Still the soldiers of Israel went on, for many days more, taking every city they came to. When they at last returned to camp, they had conquered all the southern part of Canaan, from Kadesh-barnea to Gaza.

Then the kings of the north came together, at the Waters of Merom, in the far north. They were a great host, like the sands of the sea-shore. They had a great many horses and chariots, and the soldiers of Israel did not have any horses and chariots for the battle.

God told Joshua not to be afraid. "By tomorrow at this time," He said, "I shall deliver them all into your hands."

So Joshua went with all his soldiers to the Waters of Merom. He came upon his enemies suddenly. The Lord delivered all that great host into the hands of the Israelites. The soldiers of Joshua pursued them to the city of Sidon, near the sea-coast, and to Mizpeh in the east.

Then Joshua turned back and destroyed the capital city, Hazor, where the head of these nations lived. No one in it was left alive. The other cities they did not burn, however. All the cattle and precious things that the children of Israel found in the other cities, they were allowed to keep for themselves.

Of course, the Israelites did not do this in one day. It took a long time, for every city of the land except Gibeon fought against them and was conquered. Joshua subdued thirty-one kings.

He warned the children of Israel that God did not give them the land of Canaan because they were so good that they deserved it. He destroyed those nations because of their wickedness, just as He had destroyed wicked people with a flood, and the sinners of Sodom and Gomorrah with fire. This is God's world, and He will surely punish all those who do wrong.

CHAPTER 58

Dividing the Land

Joshua 13-24; Judges 1

Although Joshua and the children of Israel had not yet conquered the whole land of Canaan, Joshua began to divide the land. He parceled it out by lot, giving each tribe a piece, according to the size of the tribe.

As I have told you before, the tribe of Levi was given forty-eight cities. Each city had a little land around it, where the Levites could pasture their cattle, but no farm land.

Joshua also appointed the six cities of refuge, where a man who had killed another without intending to do so might be safe from his pursuer. Three of these cities of refuge were on each side of the Jordan.

When all the land was conquered, Joshua called the tribes of Reuben and Gad and the half tribe of Manasseh, and he said to them, "You have kept your promise to come over the Jordan and help your brothers fight the Canaanites. Now you may go back to your homes on the other side of the Jordan."

At the same time he warned them never to forget to worship God and to obey Him.

These tribes were permitted to take along great riches in cattle, silver and gold, brass and iron, as well as beautiful clothing. All these things had been taken from the heathen who had been killed in the wars.

The Israelites had everything that the heart could wish; they had houses to live in, that they had not built; rich vineyards, which they had taken from the heathen; olive orchards, that they had not planted. They were very rich in flocks and herds, gold and silver, brass and iron.

Was it right for them to take these things away from the heathen? Yes, but only because God told them to. For many, many years God had let the heathen have all these rich blessings, but the heathen had not used God's blessings aright. They had used them for the worship of idols, and they had sinned against God in every possible way. So God told the Israelites to take the land, to enjoy it, and to worship Him.

Joshua spoke to the people and told them they must choose — would they worship the God of Abraham, Isaac and Jacob? Or would they, too, worship idols? And Joshua said, "As for me and my house, we will serve Jehovah."

Then all the people answered that they, too, would serve the Lord and Him only.

At last Joshua's life came to an end. He had lived a hundred ten years. Before he died, he reminded the children of Israel of all God's blessings, how not one thing had failed of all the good God had promised them. And he warned them that God would also surely punish them if they should disobey Him and bow down to idols. Then He would take this good land away from them, just as He had taken it away from the heathen.

The people were grateful for all that God had done for them, and they again promised to serve Him. In a city called Shiloh they set up the Tabernacle. And they were happy serving God.

After Joshua died, the children of Israel no longer had a leader. Eleazar the priest, the son of Aaron, was dead and his son was now high priest.

Some of the heathen were still left in the land, and the Israelites knew that God wanted all those people driven out. What should they do, now that they had no leader?

They did exactly the right thing — they came to God and asked Him what they should do. God told them that Judah should go first to fight against the heathen Canaanites. The tribe of Judah asked the tribe of Simeon to come with them. The Lord gave them a great victory.

After this victory, the tribes of Judah and Simeon went to fight against Hebron. This was the place where Abraham had lived many years earlier. Abraham and Sarah, Isaac and Rebekah, and Jacob and Leah were buried in the Cave of Machpelah near Hebron.

But more than four hundred years had passed since Abraham had lived in Hebron. It was now the home of a terrible race of giants called Anakims. Since the tribes of Judah and Simeon trusted the Lord to help them, God gave them the victory.

Hebron was given to Caleb, one of the men who had spied out the land of Canaan forty years before. This was his reward for trusting God.

After conquering Hebron, Judah and Simeon went to fight against the cities of Gaza, Ashkelon, and Ekron, near the Mediterranean Sea. Giants were living there, too, but Judah and Simeon conquered them with the help of God.

CHAPTER 59

Judges Rule Israel

Judges 2, 3

As long as that generation lived, who had seen the mighty works of the Lord, the children of Israel served God. But now Joshua was dead; Eleazar the priest was dead; all that generation was gone, and another generation had taken its place.

The children of Israel began to do evil in the sight of the Lord. They forsook the God of their fathers and followed the gods of the people round about them, worshipping Baal and Ashtaroth.

The anger of the Lord was aroused. He sent the heathen, who lived near by, to bother and trouble them. The Israelites were so troubled by their enemies, that at last the Lord took pity on them and sent them some judges who were good men and could rule well.

As long as the judges ruled, the people again served the Lord, and God helped them to conquer the heathen nations. But each time after the death of a judge, the people soon forgot God and worshipped the heathen idols.

Some of the heathen people remained in Canaan. In the north, around the city of Sidon and in the Lebanon mountains, the Lord left some of the Canaanites. The children of Israel lived right among these heathen people, even marrying some of them. They forgot their own God, and worshipped heathen idols. To punish them, God let the king of Mesopotamia fight against them and conquer them. For eight years the heathen king ruled over them.

Not all the children of Israel had forgotten God, however. There were some who were faithful. These cried to God for help and God sent them a deliverer. This was Othniel, Caleb's younger brother.

Othniel fought against the king of Mesopotamia and God gave him the victory. Othniel ruled Israel for forty years, until he died.

But after his death the children of Israel did evil again; and God permitted the king of Moab to come against them and to conquer them. Moab, as you will remember, is on the other side of the Jordan River, east of the Dead Sea.

The king of Moab, whose name was Eglon, ruled over the children of Israel for eighteen years. At last the people realized how wicked they had been to forget God. They turned again to Him, praying Him to help them. God heard them and gave them a deliverer, Ehud, who lived in Benjamin.

The Israelites sent Ehud to King Eglon. Ehud carried a present for the king. But Ehud meant to do more than give him the present. Before he started, he made himself a very long, sharp, two-edged dagger. He fastened it carefully to his side, under his long cloak.

When Ehud reached Moab, he found the king sitting in a cool room which he had made for himself, for he was a very fat man. After giving the present to Eglon, Ehud said to him, "I have a secret message for you, O king."

King Eglon told all the people to go out of the room, so that he could talk to Ehud alone. Ehud came close to the king, as if he were going to whisper his message so that no one else could hear.

Again Ehud said, "I have a message from God for you." At the same instant, he quickly drew his sharp dagger, and thrust it right into King Eglon's body.

Ehud went softly out of the room, shutting the doors and locking them. He hurried as fast as ever he could, and escaped to his own country.

While Ehud had been making his escape, the servants of King Eglon were waiting for him to come out of his room. They wondered and wondered why he stayed there so long. They tried the doors and found that they were locked; so they thought that he must be taking a nap and had locked the doors so that he would not be disturbed. By and by, they decided that something must be wrong. They shook the doors and called to him, but there was no answer. In the end, they found another key and opened the doors. Great was their horror to see their king lying dead upon the floor!

Meanwhile Ehud had gathered his army to go against the Moabites. Since their king was dead, the Moabites had no leader. When Ehud and his army came to fight against them, they easily gained the victory.

That was the end of the war with the Moabites. They did not trouble the Israelites again.

After this, the land of Israel had rest for eighty years.

CHAPTER 60

How Death Came to Sisera

JUDGES 4, 5

When Ehud was dead, the children of Israel did evil in the sight of the Lord again.

Then God allowed Jabin, who was king of the Canaanites far up in the north, to come down and make trouble for the Israelites. King Jabin had nine hundred chariots of iron. He oppressed the children of Israel for twenty years. Again they cried to God.

At that time Israel was ruled by a woman. The name of this woman judge was Deborah. She was a very wise and good woman. She lived in a tent under a fine palm-tree. Whenever the people of Israel needed any advice, they came to Deborah.

God told her now to send to a soldier named Barak, to tell him that God wanted him to take ten thousand soldiers and go up north to fight with Sisera, the captain of Jabin's army. God promised to give Barak the victory over Sisera.

But Barak was timid, and he said to Deborah, "I will go if you will come with me; but if you do not come, then I will not."

Deborah was a brave woman. She said, "Surely I will go with you, but it will not be you who shall have the honor of overcoming the Canaanites. God is going to give that honor to a woman."

So Barak gathered together ten thousand soldiers and went up to the Kishon river. Deborah went with him. When Sisera heard that Barak was coming to fight against him with ten thousand soldiers, he gathered his own army and his nine hundred chariots and went to the river to meet him.

God so helped the Israelites that Sisera and all his soldiers fled before them. Many were killed.

Sisera soon noticed that he was fighting a losing battle. He jumped out of his chariot and ran away till he was almost exhausted. When he was so tired that he could not run another step, he came to the tent of a country woman, all by itself. A woman named Jael lived in this tent.

Jael was not an Israelite; neither was she a Canaanite. She was a Kenite. These people lived far away in the south, near the mountains of Sinai. You remember that after Moses had run away from Pharaoh, he lived in the desert. There he had married a Kenite woman. When the children of Israel had passed through this desert, Moses had invited his brother-in-law to come along with them to guide them, because he knew the way through the desert better than Moses did. So Moses' brother-in-law had come with the Israelites, and his descendants lived among them.

Jael was a friend of the Israelites. But she said to Sisera, "Come in, my lord, and rest in my tent." She told him to lie down and she put a blanket over him.

Sisera said, "Please give me a drink of water, for I am thirsty." But Jael brought him a drink of milk.

Then Sisera said, "Stand in the door of the tent. If any soldiers come here to look for me, asking, 'Is there any man here?', you must say 'No.'"

Sisera was so tired that he soon fell into a sound sleep. When Jael saw that he was fast asleep, she took a long tent pin, like a very long nail. Softly she stole into the tent, and she hammered the spike right through his head into the ground. Sisera never awoke from that sleep.

Then Jael stood in the door of her tent. Soon Barak, the captain of the Lord's hosts, came running by, looking for Sisera.

She went out and called to him, "Come in, and I will show you the man for whom you are looking." She took him into her tent and showed him Sisera dead, with the great nail in his head.

Barak returned and told Deborah what Jael had done. Barak and Deborah sang for gladness, praising God for their great victory.

> "So let all thine enemies perish, O Jehovah,
> But let them that love Him be as the sun,
> When he goeth forth in his might."

After this victory the land had rest for forty years. Ehud had conquered the Moabites, and Deborah and Barak had defeated the Canaanites.

CHAPTER 61

Gideon, Who Saw an Angel

JUDGES 6, 7, 8

PART 1 — UNDER THE OAK TREE

By this time the children of Israel should have learned to forsake idols and to worship God only. Sad to say, they did not, for after Deborah died they did evil again in the sight of the Lord. This time the Lord let the Midianites oppress them.

The Midianites were a wandering people who did not live in one place. They were hated because of their thieving.

The Israelites had had trouble with the Midianites before, you re-member. That was two hundred years earlier, just before the Israelites crossed over the Jordan to come into the land of Canaan. King Balak had called Balaam to curse the Israelites for him, but Balaam blessed them.

Then the Midianites had been living in the land of the Amorites. Now they had come to Canaan to steal the crops of the Israelites. They had increased, in those two hundred years, to a very large nation.

They were mean thieves. Instead of settling down in one spot to cultivate their own fields, they swooped down on some weaker people, devouring all their crops. Then they would move on to another place, to steal there.

Thus it was that they treated the Israelites. They came with their cattle and their tents, as many as a cloud of grasshoppers. They laid waste the land, leaving nothing for the Israelites to eat. The children of Israel became very poor, but they were too much terrified to defend themselves, for the Midianites did not hesitate to kill any man who opposed them.

For seven long years the Midianites oppressed the children of Israel, till they did not even dare to live in their own homes any longer. Running away from the Midianites, they lived in caves and dens of the mountains.

At last they were nearly starving. In their misery they cried to God to help them. God sent them a prophet to reprove them for their idolatry.

But God was so sorry for the poor starving Israelites who had to hunt out dens in the rocks as refuge that He determined to help them. He took the form of an angel, and sat under an oak tree.

Near by was a young farmer named Gideon, who was secretly threshing some wheat, trying to hide it from the Midianites. The angel of the Lord appeared to him, saying, "Jehovah is with thee, thou mighty man of valor."

And Gideon answered, "O my Lord! If Jehovah is with us, then why have all these terrible things happened to us? Our fathers told us wonderful stories of how God brought our nation out of Egypt. But now our God has left us, and let the Midianites overcome us."

The Lord looked at Gideon and said, "Go, in this thy might, and save Israel from the Midianites. Have I not sent thee?"

Gideon was astonished. How should he, a poor farmer, save his people from the hosts of the Midianites? He managed to say, "O my Lord, how shall I save Israel? My family is the poorest in Manasseh, and I am the least important in my father's house."

But the Lord said to him, "Surely I will be with you, and you shall conquer the Midianites as easily as if they were only one man."

Gideon wanted to be sure that it was the Lord who told him these things. So he said that he would like a sign. He went home, killed a kid and boiled it, and made some little cakes of bread. He came back to the oak tree with this present.

The Lord directed him to put the bread and the meat on a rock, and to pour out the broth. Gideon did this. The angel of the Lord touched the bread and the meat with the end of a rod which he had in his hand. A fire burst out of the rock and burned the bread and the meat. At the same time, the angel passed away out of Gideon's sight.

Then Gideon knew that he had truly seen an angel of Jehovah. He was very much frightened, for he thought that he would die because he had seen an angel.

But God said to him, "Do not be afraid. You shall not die." And Gideon built an altar to God there.

Part 2 — An Overthrown Altar and a Small Army

The children of Israel had become so idolatrous that Gideon's own father was an idol worshipper. An idol of the heathen god Baal was right in his own village. By the side of the altar was the image of a goddess called Asherah, fixed in the ground by a wooden stake. The people used to worship this, too.

The night after the angel of God had appeared to Gideon, God spoke again to him, telling him to throw down the altar of Baal and cut down the Asherah beside it. Then Gideon must build an altar to the Lord on the top of the rock, and take his father's young bullock and sacrifice it on the altar, using the wood of the Asherah to build the fire.

Gideon was a brave and obedient man. He was ready to obey God, even though he knew how angry the idol-worshippers would be. He believed that God was going to help him to overcome the Midianites, and he knew that he must obey Him.

Since he knew the people would try to stop him, Gideon decided to work at night. Ten men, his servants, helped him to chop down the pole and pull down the altar of Baal. They built an altar to the true God in the place where Baal's altar had been.

In the morning, when the people of the town passed by, they were furious. Who had done this?

At last they discovered that Gideon was the one. They went to his father, threatening to kill Gideon. Gideon must have told his father that the true God had spoken to him. It had brought about a change in his heart, making him ashamed that he had worshipped the idol. He answered the people, " Are you going to defend Baal? If he be a god, let him defend himself."

When the people heard that the true God had spoken to Gideon, they were ready to help him. The spirit of God came upon him, so that he was full of courage to fight the Midianites. He sent messengers to the tribes of Manasseh and Naphtali and Asher and Zebulun, the northern tribes. Soon the soldiers came flocking to him, for they were anxious to go to fight against the Midianites, now that they had a leader to guide them.

The Midianites also were ready to fight. The Valley of Jezreel was soon filled with them. They had more than one hundred twenty thousand men, three times as many as the Israelites could gather.

Gideon wanted to be very certain that God was with him. He asked God to give him a sign. He put a fleece of wool on the ground and he said to God, "If you will truly save Israel by me, let the fleece be wet with dew tomorrow morning, and all the earth around be dry."

In the morning, Gideon found the fleece so wet that he wrung a big bowlful of water out of it. All the ground around was perfectly dry. Yet Gideon asked God to show him one more miracle. He asked that this time the fleece be left dry, and dew cover the ground.

God did as Gideon asked, for in the morning the fleece was perfectly dry and all the ground around was covered with dew. Now Gideon had to believe once and for all that God wanted him to be the leader of the Israelites against the people of Midian.

Early one morning Gideon took his thirty-two thousand soldiers and pitched camp on the south side of the Valley of Jezreel. They were on a hillside, from which they could look down into the valley where the Midianites were encamped.

Although Gideon had not even half as many soldiers as the Midianites, there were too many Israelites. If thirty-two thousand soldiers should go to fight against the Midianites, they would say that they had gained the victory, not that God had given it to them. Gideon, at the Lord's command, let the timid soldiers go home.

The soldiers were amazed. How could the Israelites gain a victory over the Midianites without a big army? If some of the Israelites should go home, how could Gideon possibly win the battle? They did not see how this could be, but twenty-two thousand of them went home, leaving only ten thousand.

Again God told Gideon there were too many. He must take them down to the brookside to drink and God would show him which ones to keep.

Gideon did so. Three hundred of the men lapped the water from their hands, as a dog laps. The others knelt and put their faces down to the water.

The Lord promised Gideon that by the three hundred men who lapped the water He would save them from the Midianites. So Gideon kept only three hundred men in his camp on the hill.

God came to Gideon at night, telling him to go down to the host of the Midianites, for He had delivered them into Gideon's hand. If he were afraid to go alone, he might take his servant with him. The things he would overhear would give him courage to fight the enemy.

Gideon and his servant slid down the hillside secretly in the dark, creeping very cautiously nearer to the camp of the Midianites.

They heard two men talking together in a tent. One man said, "I have dreamed. In my dream I saw a loaf of barley bread come tumbling down the hillside into our camp. It hit the tent and toppled it over, flat to the ground."

The other man said, "That dream has a meaning. That loaf of bread is nothing else but the sword of Gideon, for the Lord has given all the host of Midian into his hand."

That was certainly a remarkable thing for that Midianite to say. How did he know this? Perhaps he had somewhere met an Israelite soldier and had heard him say that God was going to deliver the Midianites into the hands of Gideon.

After Gideon had heard these two men talking in the tent, his courage became much greater. He and his servant crept cautiously back again into their own camp.

PART 3 — THE END OF THE THIEVES

The following night, Gideon divided his three hundred men into three companies of a hundred men each. He gave each man a pitcher, a trumpet, and a torch. He ordered the men to light the torches and to hide them in their pitchers, so that the Midianites would not see the lights.

They were now all ready. In the middle of the night Gideon and his three hundred brave men slipped down the hillside without a sound. As still as mice, they crept to the very edge of the camp of the Midianites.

One hundred men went on one side of the camp; another hundred placed themselves on the other side; and the third hundred went be-

Samson died with the Philistines. Judges 16

Boaz said to his overseer, "What young girl is this?" Ruth 2

hind the camp of the enemy. They were so quiet, that not one of those sleeping Midianites awoke to give the alarm. The whole host lay in slumber.

Then, all at once, Gideon gave the signal. He lifted his trumpet to his lips, and in an instant there rang out in the still night the terrible war cry of a trumpet. Dashing his pitcher against the stones with a tremendous crash, he seized his torch and waved it frantically above his head, shouting, "The sword of the Lord and of Gideon!"

Instantly he was answered by three hundred trumpets blaring out defiance from every quarter; and three hundred pitchers went crashing on the stones; and three hundred flaring torches streamed out in the darkness; and from three hundred throats rang the loud war cry: "The sword of the Lord and of Gideon."

The dazed Midianites awoke with terror. They jumped up, and rushed to their tent-doors. On every side they saw streaming torches, lighting up the faces of strange soldiers. On every side they heard the war cry of the trumpets, and yells of the Israelite soldiers, "The sword of the Lord and of Gideon."

Stupid with sleep and terror, they thought that a tremendous host had come upon them. Their first thought was to save themselves. In their confusion and fear, they seized their swords and spears and hit at everything around them. They had no time to get lights, and in the darkness they could not tell friend from foe. They slashed this way and that, killing each other in the terrible tumult.

Gideon hurried to send messengers to all the soldiers whom he had sent home, telling them to come and pursue the fleeing Midianites. The Israelite army hurried after their enemies until they reached the Jordan River.

One hundred twenty thousand Midianites had already fallen by the sword. They had killed each other in their confusion. On the other side of the river there were left only fifteen thousand Midianites with their kings, Zebah and Zalmunna. Gideon did not want to leave any of these people alive to trouble the Israelites; so he crossed the Jordan after them.

Gideon's soldiers had to pass through a city called Succoth. They were faint with hunger, for they had been fighting all the night. Gideon asked the men of the city to give them bread to eat. The people of Succoth were Israelites, and the soldiers were fighting to drive away the thieving Midianites from them. Yet the princes of the city refused them bread, saying, "You have not yet caught Zebah and Zalmunna, so why should we feed your soldiers?"

Gideon was angered by this refusal and he promised to punish them. The people of Penuel, the next town the army passed through, treated them in the same way. Gideon promised to punish them, too.

Soon the Israelite army overtook the fifteen thousand Midianites and conquered them. The kings, Zebah and Zalmunna, escaped, only to be brought back in chains by Gideon.

The Israelites took away the golden ear-rings of all the Midianites and the ornaments of their camels' necks. There was more than eight thousand dollars' worth of gold in the ear-rings alone.

Before the sun rose, Gideon and his men came back to the city of Succoth, leading the two kings of the Midianites, whom the elders of the city thought he could not capture. His soldiers gave each of the seventy-seven men a thrashing with thorns and briers, to punish them for refusing to give bread to his faint and hungry soldiers.

Then Gideon went on to Penuel and pulled down their tower, because these people also had refused to help the army of the Lord.

In this one night, by the help of the Lord, Gideon and his soldiers routed that immense host of more than one hundred twenty thousand Midianites. The men of Israel were so much pleased with Gideon, that they wanted to make him their ruler. But Gideon said that neither he nor his sons would rule over Israel. God must be their Lord.

And the land had rest forty years in the days of Gideon.

CHAPTER 62

Samson

JUDGES 13-16

PART 1 — A HARD RIDDLE

After the death of Gideon the children of Israel served idols again. They served not only Baal and Asherah, but they worshipped the gods of all the heathen peoples around them. They forgot their own God, while they were sacrificing to the fish-god of the Philistines, and the burning idol, Moloch.

The anger of God was great, because of their faithlessness. He let the heathen nations trouble the Israelites for many years.

At last the children of Israel cried to the Lord to deliver them. The Lord reminded them that, although He had delivered them many times before, still they served idols. Why did they not cry to their idols, and let them deliver them?

But the children of Israel did not give up. They were truly sorry that they had sinned, and they prayed that the Lord would deliver them once more. They put away their idols and served the Lord.

It was now about eighty years since Gideon had died. Seven different judges had ruled, but now there was no law in the land. Every man did what he pleased, for these were wild, rough times. The people had become almost like heathen people.

In these troubled days, there was a man of the tribe of Dan whose name was Manoah. He and his wife had no child.

One day when Manoah's wife was all alone, an angel of the Lord came to her saying she was to have a son, who was to be given to God from his birth. His hair must never be cut and he should never drink wine. He should begin to deliver Israel from the Philistines when he grew up.

It was the Philistines who now were troubling the Israelites. They lived in the west, near the shore of the Mediterranean Sea. The cities of Gath and Gaza and Lachish were Philistine cities.

In the next year the baby was born to Manoah and his wife. The father and mother called him Samson. As the boy grew up, he became very strong.

One day, as Samson was walking alone, a lion came near him. Although the lion is a strong, fierce animal, Samson took hold of that lion and tore him to pieces with his bare hands.

Soon after this, Samson fell in love with a Philistine woman. He told his father and mother that he wanted to marry her. They did not like to have him marry a heathen woman, but at last they gave in. They all went together to the country of the Philistines to visit the woman.

It was a great mistake for Samson to marry a heathen woman. It caused him a great deal of trouble. But God used the matter to help the Israelites.

On the way home from visiting the Philistine woman. Samson turned aside to look at the body of the lion he had killed. He found that a swarm of bees had made a hive in the lion's dried-up body. Samson took some of the honey from the hive and ate it, and gave some to his father and mother.

When Samson came down to the country of the Philistines again, he made a fine wedding feast. Thirty young men were invited to this party, which lasted a whole week.

At this party, everyone told riddles. Samson told a riddle about the lion and the honey. He said if they could guess his riddle before the party ended, he would give them thirty shirts and thirty robes. If they could not guess it by that time, they must give him thirty shirts and thirty robes.

They all agreed to this. Then Samson told them the riddle:

"Out of the eater came forth food,
And out of the strong came forth sweetness."

The young men guessed and guessed for three whole days, but they could not give the right answer. They began to be afraid they could never guess it, but they did not want to give Samson the thirty shirts and robes they had promised.

On the last day of the party they came to Samson's wife. They said, "You must coax your husband to tell you the answer to that riddle, and then you must tell us. If you will not do so, we will come and burn you and all your family. Did you invite us to this party just to make us poor?" You see what wicked people they were!

Samson's wife came to him. She began to cry, "You do not love me at all! You hate me, because you have given a riddle to my people and not told me the answer!"

Samson answered, "But I have not told my father and mother, and why should I tell you?"

But his wife only kept wailing, "You do not love me at all, or you would tell me the answer."

At last Samson was so tired of her teasing that he told her. She in turn told the answer to the thirty young men. They came to Samson and boasted, "We know that riddle now. What is sweeter than honey, and what is stronger than a lion?"

Samson immediately saw that they had made his wife tell them, because they could never have guessed it by themselves; and he spoke angrily, "If you had not ploughed with my heifer, you would not have found out my riddle."

Samson could hardly control his wrath, but he had to keep his promise to give them thirty shirts and thirty robes. Where should he get so many garments? He did not have money enough to buy them. He went to the Philistine city of Ashkelon and killed thirty Philistines and gave their clothes to the young men.

That was a dreadful thing to do, but it helped the Israelites. God had told Samson's mother that Samson was to begin to deliver his people from the Philistines. That was what God had given Samson his great strength for.

PART 2 — A ONE-MAN BATTLE

After Samson had given the thirty changes of garments to the young men, he went home still in a great rage. He left behind his wife, who had betrayed him. Her father, seeing that Samson did not seem to love her any longer, gave her to another man.

After some time Samson stopped being angry with her. He went to her father's house, taking a little kid along for a present to his wife. When he reached the house, he was surprised to find that his father-in-law would not let him see his wife. You can imagine how he felt when he learned what had happened.

He wanted revenge. He caught three hundred foxes. Then he turned them tail to tail, tying the two tails together with a piece of dry wood between them. Setting the wood on fire, he let the foxes go into the standing grain of the Philistines. The grainfields were burned. The vineyards and the olive orchards were destroyed, too.

When the Philistines saw all their grain burned, and their vineyards and olive orchards on fire, they were furious. Someone said that Samson had done it because his father-in-law had given his wife to another man.

The Philistines could not punish Samson, for he was too strong. They went to his father-in-law's house and burned Samson's wife and her father. Probably they set fire to the house at night when everyone was asleep.

But Samson was still more angry when he found out that the Philistines had killed his wife and his father-in-law. He went out and fought against them, killing a great many. Finally, in disgust with the heathen Philistines, he went back to his own country Judah and lived in a secret cave on the top of a high rock called Etham.

The Philistines went up into Judah and hunted for Samson. The men of Judah were much afraid of such wild and rough people. They asked, "What have you come here for?"

"We have come to catch Samson, to pay him back for the way he has treated us," answered the Philistines.

When the men of Judah heard the Philistines say that they wanted only Samson and no one else, then they went to the cave in the rock to find him. The men of Judah knew that Samson was very strong, and that no single man, not even three or four men, could handle him. So three thousand of them went.

Without much difficulty they found him. "Why have you done all these things to the Philistines?" they asked. "Don't you see that you have made them angry, and that means trouble for us?"

Samson must have laughed to himself when he heard them say that all three thousand of them had come to bind him. He told them they might tie him up. They bound his legs and arms with two new ropes which they wound around him so that he could not get away. Then they brought him down to the Philistines.

More than a thousand Philistines were watching to see if the men of Judah could really catch and bind Samson. When they saw him securely bound, they set up a loud shout of triumph.

When Samson heard that shout, the spirit of the Lord came upon him and gave him mighty strength. He snapped off those strong new ropes as if they had been only threads burned in the fire.

Samson saw the jaw-bone of an ass lying on the ground. He made one leap and picked it up. Striking right and left, as fast as he could make his mighty arms fly, he dashed into the midst of the Philistines. The force of those blows was so great that the men who were struck fell down dead, one on top of another.

Of course, the Philistines ran in every direction. They were in such a hurry that they stumbled over each other and fell. Samson easily caught up with them and rained blows on their heads and shoulders, thick and fast.

At last he stopped, drew a long breath, and looked about him. All around there were heaps of dead men. Samson counted them. You will hardly believe that there were a thousand men in those great heaps. It was God who gave Samson his great strength so that he could deliver the children of Israel from their enemies.

I do not think there has ever been another such fight as this, when one man alone, without the usual weapons, killed a thousand men.

After this great fight Samson was so thirsty that he thought he would die for lack of water, or that the Philistines would capture him in his weakness. He called upon God in his trouble and God made a spring of delicious cool water bubble up out of a hollow place in the ground. If you were to go to that country, you could see the same spring that God sent to take care of the man who trusted in Him.

Some time after this, Samson went again to the country of the Philistines, to the city of Gaza. Like most cities of that time, Gaza was a walled town with heavy gates.

Someone told the city rulers that Samson had come into the town that afternoon. They closed and locked the gates. "Now," people said, "we have caught him. He cannot get out. In the morning when he tries to go out, we will kill him." So they set watchers by the city gates.

But in the middle of the night, Samson got up to go home. Finding the gates shut and locked, he pulled up the posts that the gates were fastened to, and he put the two heavy gates, with the posts and the bar and all, upon his shoulders. He carried them thirty miles away to a hill near Hebron in his own country.

CHAPTER 63

Samson Captured

JUDGES 16

PART 1 — DELILAH

Some time after this, Samson again went into the country of the Philistines. He saw another Philistine woman with whom he fell in love. Her name was Delilah.

The lords of the Philistines came to Delilah one day, when Samson was not around, and they said to her, "See if you can persuade him to tell you what makes him so strong. Find out from him if there is any way in which we can bind him, so that he cannot break the ropes. If you will do this, each of us will give you eleven hundred pieces of silver."

If Delilah had been a good woman, and if she had loved Samson, she would have refused. She knew that the Philistines would torture and kill Samson if they found out how to take his great strength. But she was not a good woman. She cared more for the eleven hundred pieces of silver than she did for Samson.

When she was alone with him, she said to Samson, "Tell me where your great strength lies, and how it could be taken away from you."

Samson did not tell her the truth. "If they bind me with seven green twigs that were never dried, then I will be weak, just like other men," he said.

Delilah told the lords of the Philistines what Samson had said. They brought to her seven green twigs that had never been dried, and hid themselves in the room. Delilah bound Samson with the twigs and cried, "The Philistines are coming!"

Samson jumped up, threw out his arms, and broke the seven green twigs as quickly as a string is broken when it touches the fire.

Delilah saw that he had not told her the truth. Again she coaxed him to tell her the truth. But Samson did not tell her the truth. Instead he said, "If they bind me with new ropes that have never been used, then I shall be as weak as other men."

So Delilah took some new ropes that had never been used, and she bound him with them. This time, also, there were men hidden in the room. When Samson was securely tied, she called, "The Philistines are coming!"

Samson jumped up and threw out his arms. The new ropes broke like a thread.

Delilah was provoked. "You have told me lies again. You are only making fun of me. Now tell me truly how you can be bound."

Samson answered, "When you are weaving your cloth, you must weave the seven locks of my long hair in the web you are weaving."

While Samson lay down with his head close to the web, Delilah began to weave. Back and forth her shuttle went, weaving Samson's long hair into her cloth. After she had woven his long hair as part of the cloth in her loom, she cried, "Samson, Samson, the Philistines are coming!"

Samson woke up and rushed out. He carried along with him by his hair the heavy loom, and the pin and beam. Delilah saw that he had again deceived her. He was as strong as ever.

"How can you say that you love me," she reproached him, "when you are telling me lies all the time? You have mocked me three times, and you have not really told me what makes you so strong."

Samson very well knew that he ought not to tell her. God had given him his great strength so that he could help his countrymen to overcome the cruel Philistines. If he should tell Delilah the secret, she would surely tell it to the lords of the Philistines.

Part 2 — The Captive

Day after day Delilah teased and tormented Samson to tell her what gave him his strength. She wanted those eleven hundred pieces of silver that each of the lords of the Philistines had promised her. She did not care about Samson.

She kept it up until Samson was tired to death of her teasing. At last he thought he could not stand it any longer, and he explained that his hair had never been cut, for he had been a Nazarite to God ever since his birth. If his hair were cut, then he would lose his strength and become weak, just as other men.

Delilah instantly knew that he had told her the truth this time. She sent to the lords of the Philistines, saying, "He has told me the secret this time. Come up once more, for he has told me how to take away his strength."

The lords came up once more, taking along the money for Delilah. She hid a barber in the house, and then made Samson go to sleep with his head in her lap.

When she saw that he was sleeping soundly, she beckoned to the barber. He came in very softly and cut off the seven locks of Samson's hair. Then Delilah called out loudly: "Samson, Samson, wake up, the Philistines are coming!"

Samson awoke out of his sleep, and he said to himself, "I will go out as I did the other times, and shake myself." He did not know that God had left him. He lost his great strength when he broke God's command that his hair should never be cut.

It did not take the Philistines long to capture him, for now he was as weak as other men. His cruel masters put out his eyes.

Then they took him down to Gaza, the very town whose gates he had carried off. They bound him with brass chains and made him grind grain in the prison house.

Poor Samson! He was blind, and his strength was gone. All day long he was forced to walk round and round, turning the mill that ground grain!

But God had not left him forever. His hair began to grow again, and with it his strength returned.

The Philistines prepared to give a big feast. They wanted to offer a great sacrifice to their fish-god Dagon, for they thought it was he who had helped them to capture Samson.

This big feast was held in the temple of Dagon. There were about six thousand people in the place, eating and drinking and singing to celebrate their victory over their enemy Samson.

While they were having a good time, they said, "Let us bring Samson here out of the prison, so that we can mock him."

As poor blind Samson stumbled along, led by a little boy, the people set up a shout of derision. If he fell over something, the people screamed with laughter.

The temple was full of men and women. Three thousand of them sat on the flat roof, looking down to see Samson. After a time, he asked the little boy who led him to put his hands on the pillars that held up the roof of the house, so that he could lean on them.

Then he prayed from the depths of his heart, "O Lord God, strengthen me, I pray thee, only this once, that I may be avenged of the Philistines for my two eyes."

He took hold of the two middle pillars which held up the roof, one with his right hand, and one with his left. Then he said, "Let me die with the Philistines." He put forth all his strength, and bowed himself and pulled with all his might. The pillars creaked and staggered. Down they came with a mighty crash, bringing the roof with them. All the people on the roof tumbled with shrieks and screams on those who were below, crushing them.

Samson died with the Philistines. In his death, he killed a greater number of his enemies than in his life.

Poor Samson had had a sad and unhappy life, but he had helped Israel by destroying very many of the Philistines. For a time they did not trouble the Israelites.

If it seems dreadful that the Israelites were commanded to kill so many of the heathen people, we must remember that the only knowledge of the true God was with the Jewish people. If they had been overcome by the heathen, or if they had turned to worshipping their idols, the knowledge of the true God would have been lost for the entire world.

God did not want this to happen.

The Israelites often disobeyed Him, marrying the heathen and worshipping idols. They turned back to Him each time, and He sent them a judge to rule over them. In the four hundred years after Joshua's death fifteen judges ruled over Israel.

CHAPTER 64

Ruth's Choice

RUTH

PART 1 — A SAD STORY

You must not think that all the people forsook God to worship idols in the days of the judges. No, indeed; there were many who tried to obey God, and to live just as God had commanded them to. I am now going to tell you a story about some of these God-fearing people.

When the judges ruled, there lived in the land of Israel a man whose name was Elimelech. He was a good man, who truly worshipped God and would have nothing to do with idols.

Elimelech was married to a sweet wife, Naomi, which means *pleasant.* They had two sons, named Mahlon and Chilion, who had grown up to be fine young men.

They were a very happy family living in Bethlehem, on the land that had been given to their forefathers when Joshua had parceled out the land of Canaan to the children of Israel.

After a time there came several bad years, when nothing would grow. So little rain fell that there was a famine in the land. Across the Jordan River, in the land of Moab, there was no famine.

Elimelech and his wife, after talking things over between themselves, thought it would be better to leave Bethlehem for a time, and live in Moab until better times should come.

They did not sell their own land in Bethlehem, for God did not allow any of the Israelites to sell their land. It always remained in the same family, descending from father to son. They probably rented their land to another farmer.

After Elimelech's family had lived in Moab for a time, the father died. This was very sad for Naomi, but she still had her two sons, who were able to take care of their mother.

By and by Mahlon and Chilion married two young women of Moab. Their names were Ruth and Orpah.

The two young women were heathen when they married Mahlon and Chilion. But when they lived in Naomi's family and saw the whole family worshipping the true God, and when they heard them telling about the wonderful acts of God, and when they saw how good Mahlon and Chilion were, and what a sweet lady Naomi was, they made up their minds that they, too, would worship the true God.

At last, when they had been in Moab about ten years, a terrible trouble came upon this family. First one of the sons died, and then the other. Poor Naomi had lost her husband and both of her sons. Ruth and Orpah were left widows.

Soon afterwards, Naomi heard that God had sent plentiful rains to the land of Israel. The famine was over. She had lost her husband and her sons, and she longed to go back home so that she might at least be among her own people, her friends and relatives.

One day she told her two daughters-in-law that she had decided to go back again to Bethlehem, in the land of Judah.

Ruth and Orpah said that they would go with her. The three started to walk to Bethlehem. It was several days' journey. After they had gone some distance, Naomi said to her two daughters-in-law, "Thank you very much for walking so far with me. Now each of you had better go home to her mother's house.

"I pray that God will be kind to you, as you have been to me, and to my dead sons. May God give you other husbands so that you may be happy again."

Ruth and Orpah began to cry. They said, "No, but we will go on with you to your country."

Naomi said, "No, my daughters; it is better for you to go back to your own country. It makes me feel sad for your sakes that God has sent me so much trouble. Return to your home country."

Then both of them began to cry again. After a while, Orpah dried her eyes, kissed her mother-in-law good-bye, and started to go back to her native land.

Naomi suggested to Ruth, "See, your sister-in-law has gone back to her own people and her own gods. Now you had better return."

But Ruth only cried the harder. She threw her arms around her mother-in-law, holding her tight, and said, "Do not tell me to leave you. I love you, and I want to stay with you. Where you go I will go, where you live I will live; your people shall be my people, and your God shall be my God. Nothing but death will ever part us."

When Naomi saw that Ruth no longer wanted to be a heathen but that she truly wanted to become an Israelite, she stopped trying to persuade her to go back.

The two went on together. They crossed the Jordan River and walked until they came to Bethlehem.

PART 2 — A HAPPY ENDING

You must remember that there was no postman to carry letters in those days. Probably the people of Bethlehem had heard very little about Elimelech and Naomi since they had left Bethlehem ten years earlier. When they saw the two women, Ruth and Naomi, walking into town one warm evening, they gathered around them; and when they saw the older lady looking sad and tired, they said, "Can this be Naomi, who left here ten years ago, so happy with her splendid husband and her two fine sons?"

And Naomi said, "Do not call me Naomi, which means *pleasant,* but call me Mara, which means *bitter.* I have had bitter trouble since I left here. I went out with my husband and my two sons, but my husband and my sons are dead, and now I have come back alone."

Such bad news shocked the people. They were very kind to Naomi. They welcomed Ruth for Naomi's sake. So Ruth and Naomi went to live in the house where Naomi had lived with her family.

Ruth was not the only person who had left the Canaanites to join the people of God. Do you remember Rahab, who hid the spies when Joshua sent them to look over the city of Jericho? And do you remember that when the soldiers destroyed the city, they saved Rahab and her family, and that she lived among the Israelites after that?

After a time, Rahab had married a fine Israelite man and had children. When they grew up, Rahab's children married Israelites and worshipped the true God. At the time of Ruth and Naomi, one of Rahab's descendants, named Boaz, was a rich and important man in Bethlehem. He was a near relative of Naomi's husband.

It was just the time of the barley harvest when Ruth and Naomi returned. All the fields around Bethlehem were filled with reapers.

As the reapers cut down the barley and tied it into sheaves, working very fast to get over the big field, some stalks of barley fell on the ground. The reapers did not pick up all these fallen stalks. Long ago, in Moses' time, God had given a law that when the reapers went over a field, they should not go over it a second time to gather up the stalks which fell to the ground. They should leave those for the poor people.

When Ruth saw all the other young women going out to glean barley after the reapers, she asked Naomi to let her go, too. She happened to choose Boaz' field in which to glean.

Boaz had hired a great many reapers to harvest his fields. A number of young women were gleaning after the reapers. He came one day to see how his men were getting along. He said to them, "The Lord be with you." They answered, "The Lord bless thee." Was not that a beautiful way for them to greet one another? Surely these people were true worshippers of God.

After he had greeted the reapers, Boaz saw Ruth among the gleaners. He said to his overseer, "What young girl is this?"

"This is the Moabite girl who came back with Naomi," replied the man. "She asked me if she could glean after the reapers."

Then Boaz went to Ruth and spoke very kindly to her, giving her permission to glean in his fields all the time and to drink of the fresh water that his young men drew.

When Ruth heard Boaz speaking to her in so friendly a way, she bowed herself down to the ground, asking why he should be so kind to her, a stranger.

He said, "I have heard how kind you have been to Naomi and how you have come to live here. The Lord will reward you for trusting yourself under His wings." Perhaps Boaz was thinking of how Rahab, too, had left heathenism.

At dinner time Boaz gave Ruth a special invitation to sit down with the reapers. He passed her some of the food, and she ate it. After she had left the table, Boaz said to the reapers, "Let her glean wherever she wants, and purposely let some stalks fall from the bundle for her."

Ruth gleaned until evening. She took her barley home to her mother-in-law. Naomi said to her, "Where have you gleaned today?"

"The name of the man is Boaz," Ruth said.

Naomi was delighted to think that God had sent her into the field of Boaz, their cousin. She told Ruth to stay in his fields to glean.

It was the custom at that time among the Israelites that when a man died, some one who was a near relative should marry his wife. When Boaz saw the beautiful Ruth gleaning in his fields day after day, he fell in love with her. He asked her to become his wife.

Ruth married Boaz, and went to live in his beautiful house. Naomi was very much pleased.

After a time a little son was born to Ruth and Boaz. He was named Obed. Naomi took him in her arms. All her neighbors came to see the baby, and they said, "Blessed be the Lord who in your old age has given you this child to love — this child of your daughter-in-law, who is better to you than seven sons."

This child was the grandfather of David. In the course of time, from his family came Jesus, the Savior.